GRAPHIC LIBRARY

GRAPHIC SCIENCE

# INVESTIGATING THE SCIENTIFIC METHOD WITH MAX AXIOM SUPER SCIENTIST

by Donald B. Lemke
illustrated by Tod Smith and Al Milgrom

Consultant:
Leslie Flynn, PhD
Science Education, Chemistry
University of Minnesota

Capstone press
Mankato, Minnesota

Graphic Library is published by Capstone Press,
151 Good Counsel Drive, P.O. Box 669, Mankato, Minnesota 56002.
www.capstonepress.com


Printed in the United States of America

1 2 3 4 5 6 13 12 11 10 09 08

*Library of Congress Cataloging-in-Publication Data*

Lemke, Donald B.
Investigating the scientific method with Max Axiom, super scientist / by Donald B. Lemke; illustrated by Tod Smith and Al Milgrom.
p. cm. — (Graphic library. Graphic science)
Summary: "In graphic novel format, follows the adventures of Max Axiom as he explains the scientific method" — Provided by publisher.
Includes bibliographical references and index.
ISBN-13: 978-1-4296-1329-3 (hardcover)
ISBN-10: 1-4296-1329-7 (hardcover)
ISBN-13: 978-1-4296-1760-4 (softcover pbk.)
ISBN-10: 1-4296-1760-8 (softcover pbk.)
1. Science — Methodology — Juvenile literature. I. Smith, Tod, ill. II. Milgrom, Al, ill. III. Title. IV. Series.
Q175.2.L46 2008
507.2 — dc22 2007022792

*Art Director and Designer*
Bob Lentz

*Cover Artist*
Tod Smith

*Colorist*
Krista Ward

*Editor*
Christopher L. Harbo

Photo illustration credits: Alamy/Visual & Written SL, 15

# TABLE OF CONTENTS

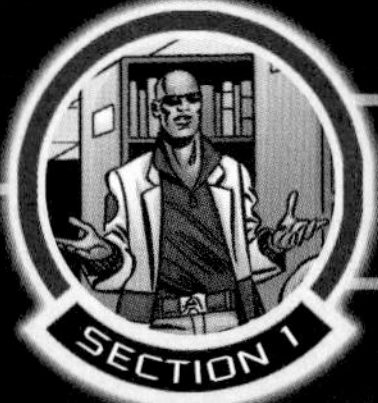
SECTION 1



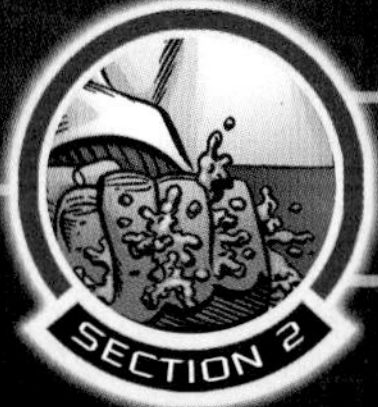
SECTION 2



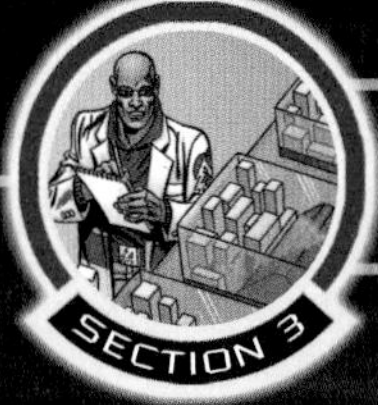
SECTION 3



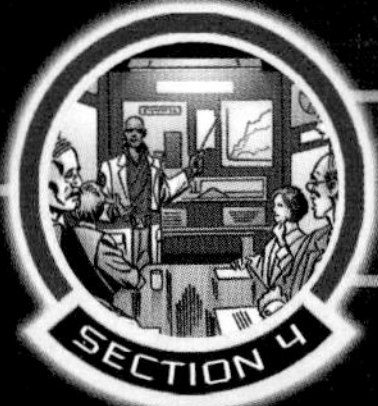
SECTION 4

## SECTION 1 A WORLD OF QUESTIONS

*Inside his high-tech laboratory, Super Scientist Max Axiom receives an important video message.*

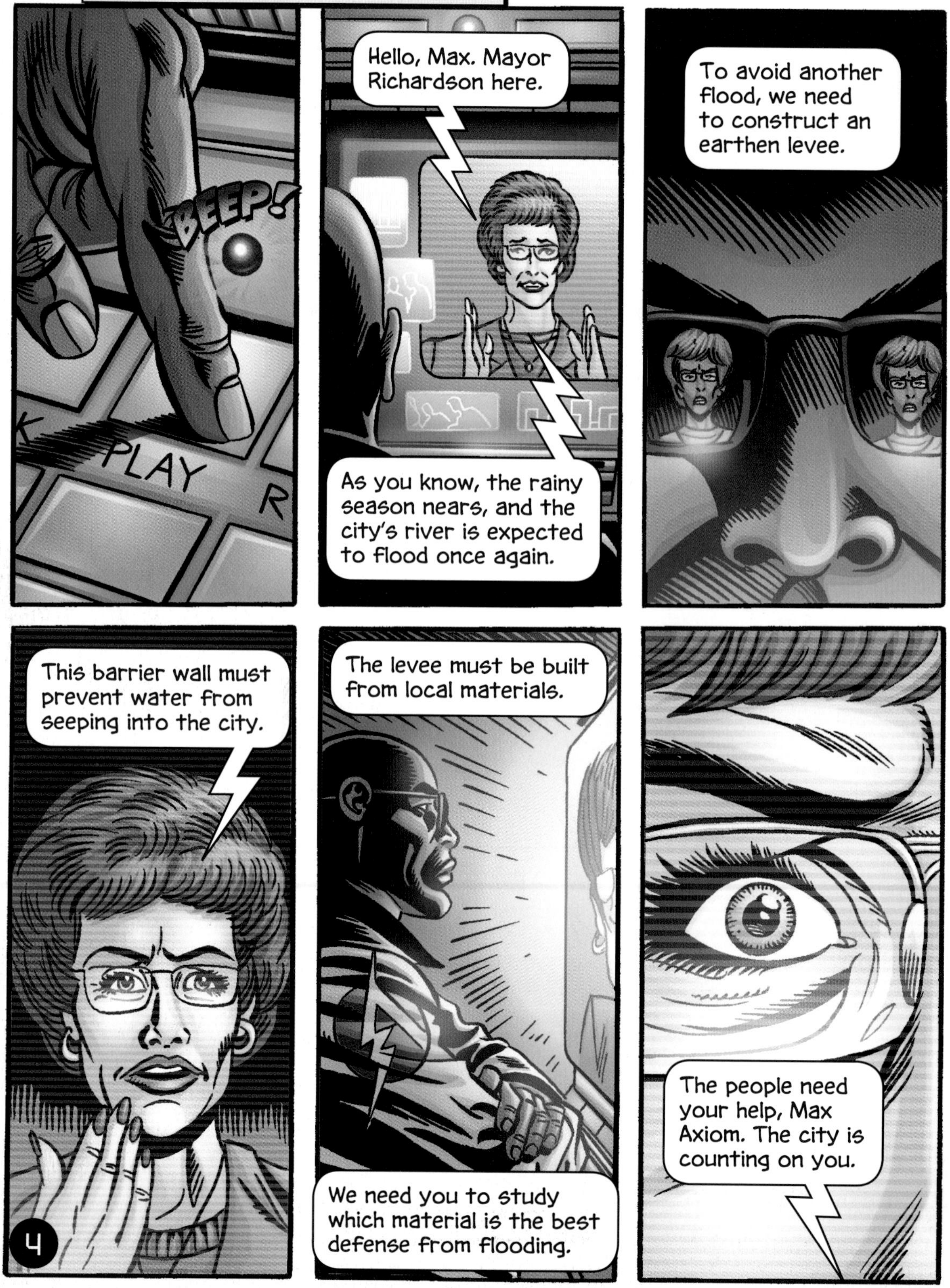
BEEP!
PLAY
Hello, Max. Mayor Richardson here.
As you know, the rainy season nears, and the city's river is expected to flood once again.
To avoid another flood, we need to construct an earthen levee.
This barrier wall must prevent water from seeping into the city.
The levee must be built from local materials.
We need you to study which material is the best defense from flooding.
The people need your help, Max Axiom. The city is counting on you.

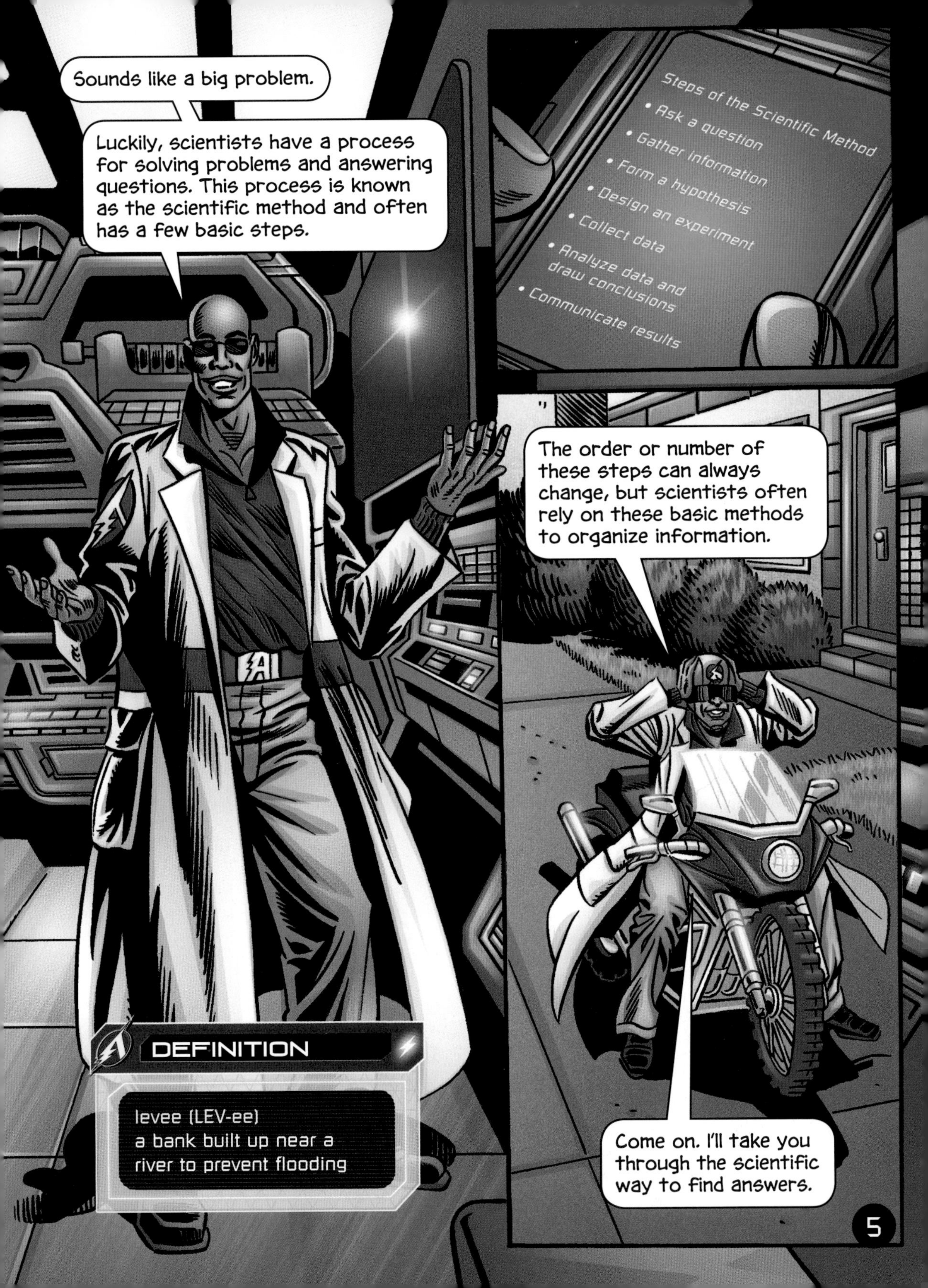

Sounds like a big problem.
Luckily, scientists have a process for solving problems and answering questions. This process is known as the scientific method and often has a few basic steps.
Steps of the Scientific Method
• Ask a question
• Gather information
• Form a hypothesis
• Design an experiment
• Collect data
• Analyze data and draw conclusions
• Communicate results
The order or number of these steps can always change, but scientists often rely on these basic methods to organize information.
Come on. I'll take you through the scientific way to find answers.
DEFINITION
levee (LEV-ee)
a bank built up near a river to prevent flooding

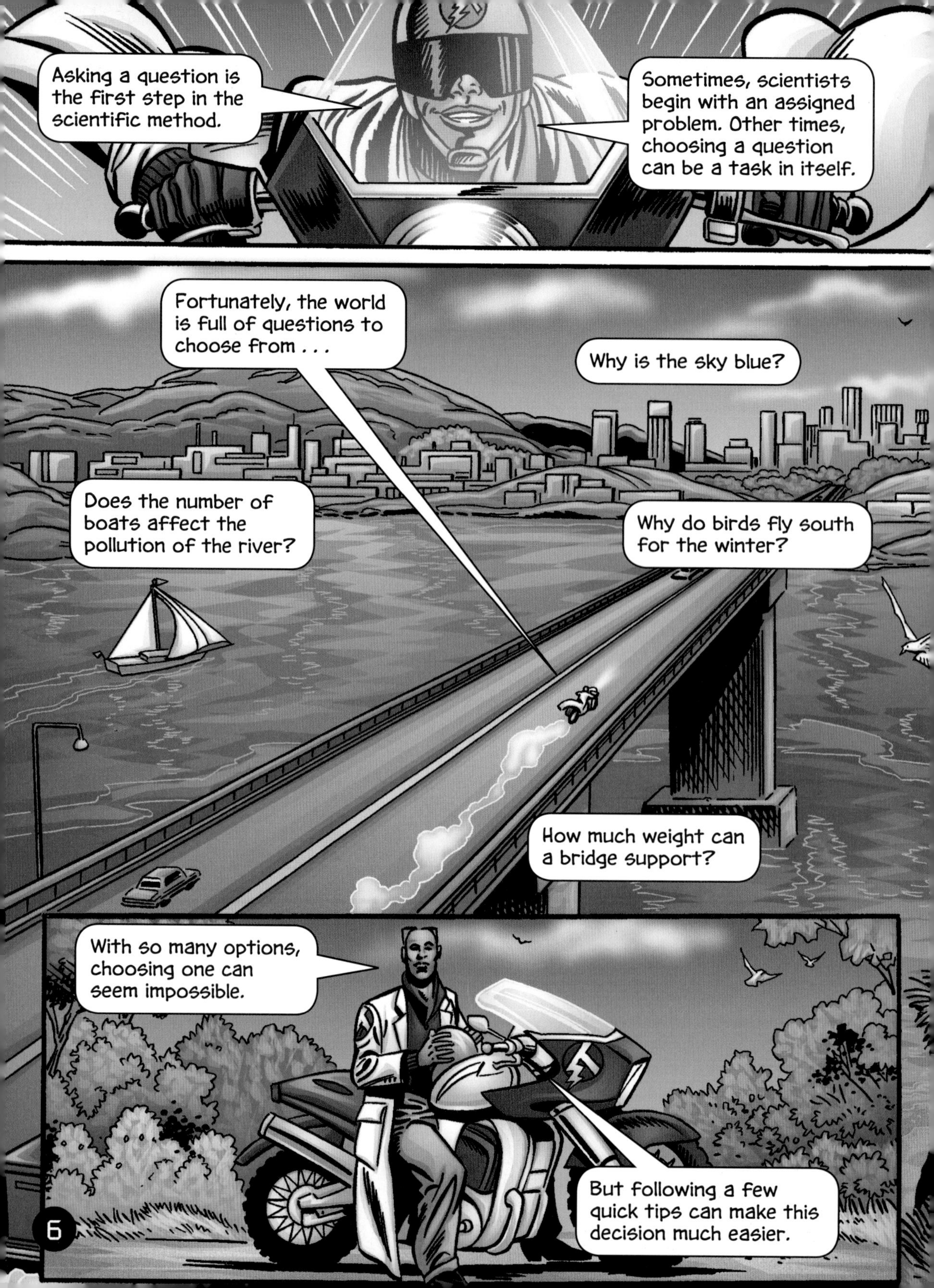
Asking a question is the first step in the scientific method.
Sometimes, scientists begin with an assigned problem. Other times, choosing a question can be a task in itself.
Fortunately, the world is full of questions to choose from . . .
Why is the sky blue?
Does the number of boats affect the pollution of the river?
Why do birds fly south for the winter?
How much weight can a bridge support?
With so many options, choosing one can seem impossible.
But following a few quick tips can make this decision much easier.

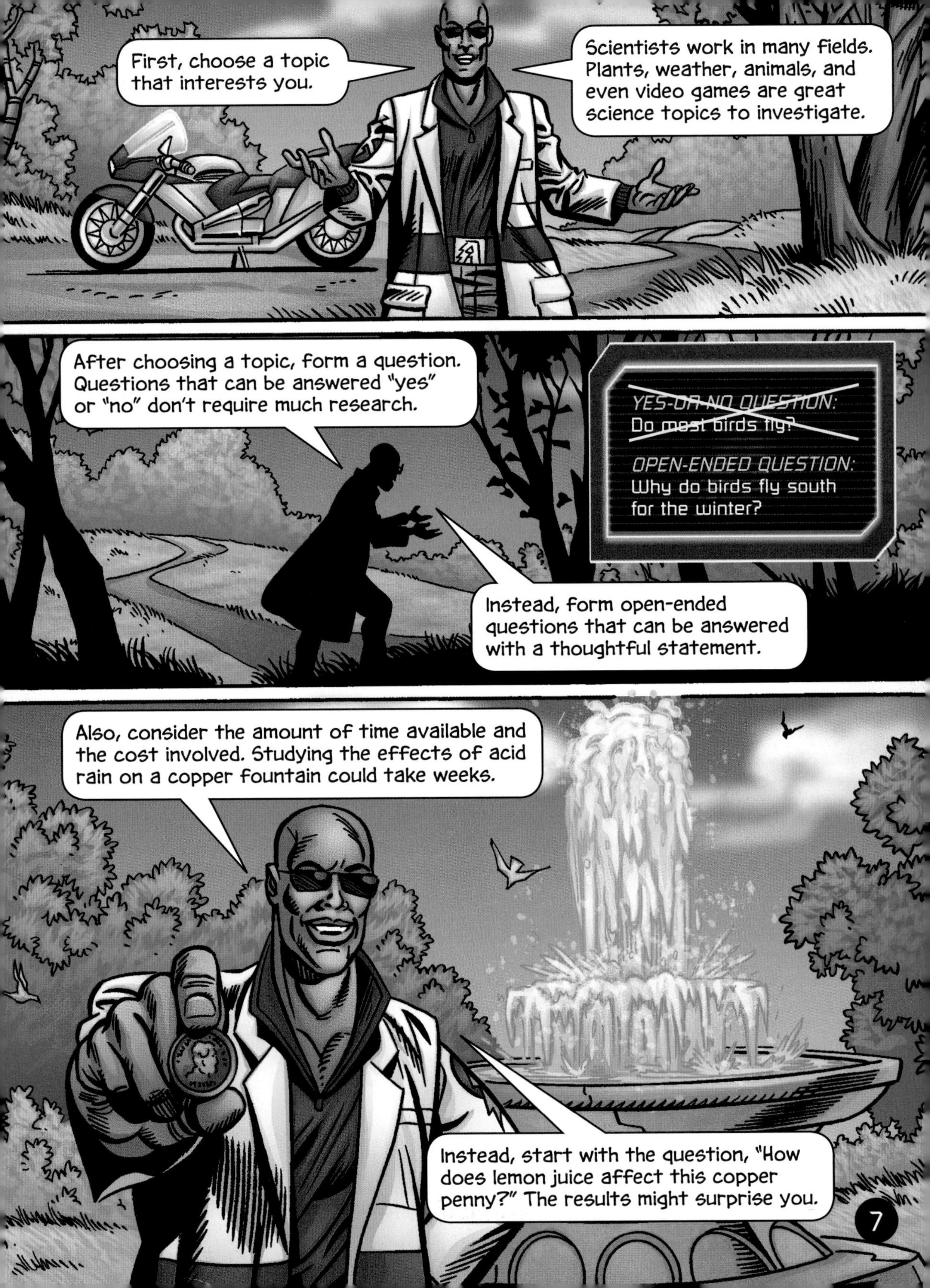
First, choose a topic that interests you.
Scientists work in many fields. Plants, weather, animals, and even video games are great science topics to investigate.
After choosing a topic, form a question. Questions that can be answered "yes" or "no" don't require much research.
YES-OR-NO QUESTION:
Do most birds fly?
OPEN-ENDED QUESTION:
Why do birds fly south for the winter?
Instead, form open-ended questions that can be answered with a thoughtful statement.
Also, consider the amount of time available and the cost involved. Studying the effects of acid rain on a copper fountain could take weeks.
Instead, start with the question, "How does lemon juice affect this copper penny?" The results might surprise you.

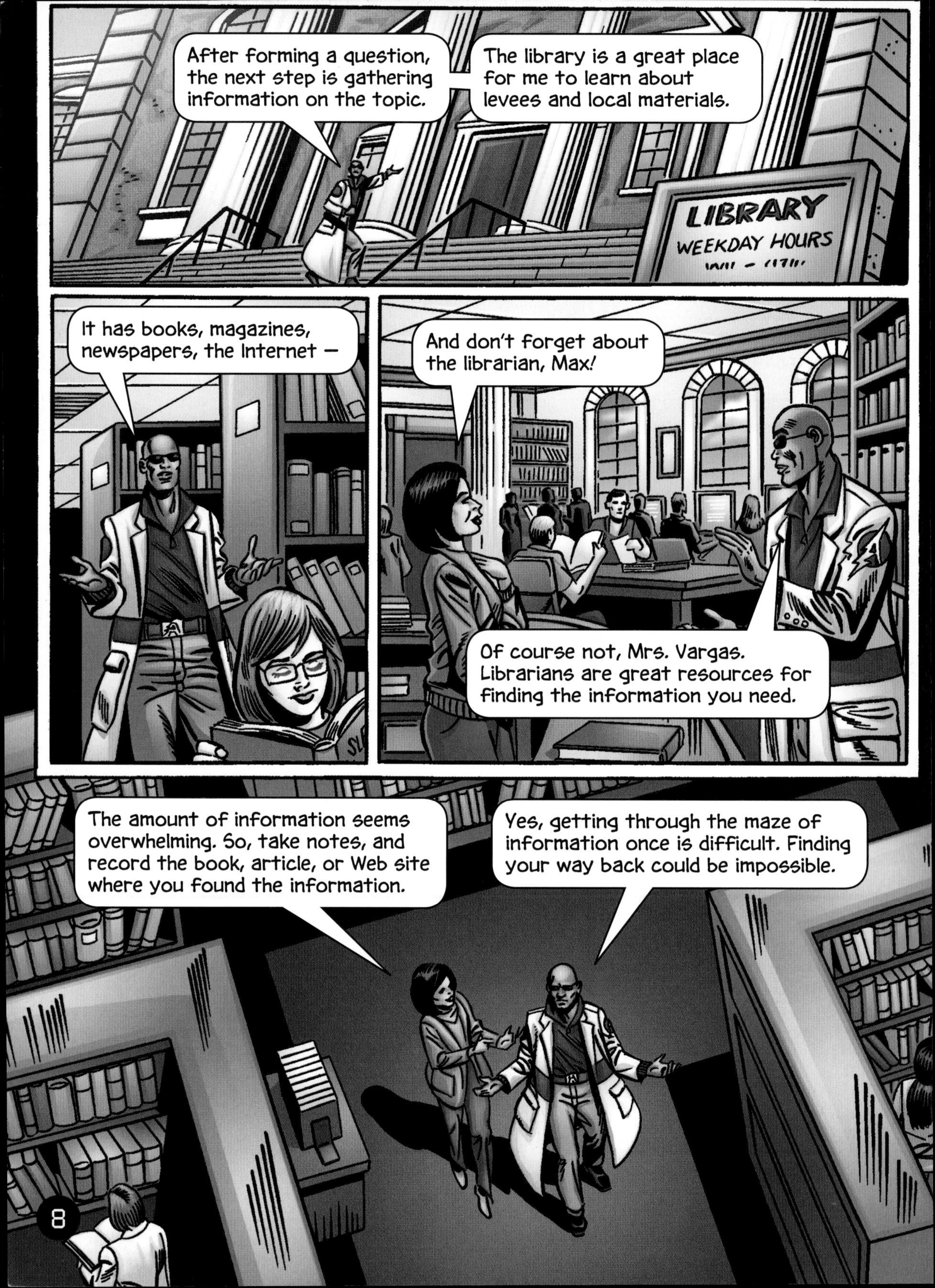
After forming a question, the next step is gathering information on the topic.
The library is a great place for me to learn about levees and local materials.
LIBRARY
WEEKDAY HOURS
It has books, magazines, newspapers, the Internet —
And don't forget about the librarian, Max!
Of course not, Mrs. Vargas. Librarians are great resources for finding the information you need.
The amount of information seems overwhelming. So, take notes, and record the book, article, or Web site where you found the information.
Yes, getting through the maze of information once is difficult. Finding your way back could be impossible.

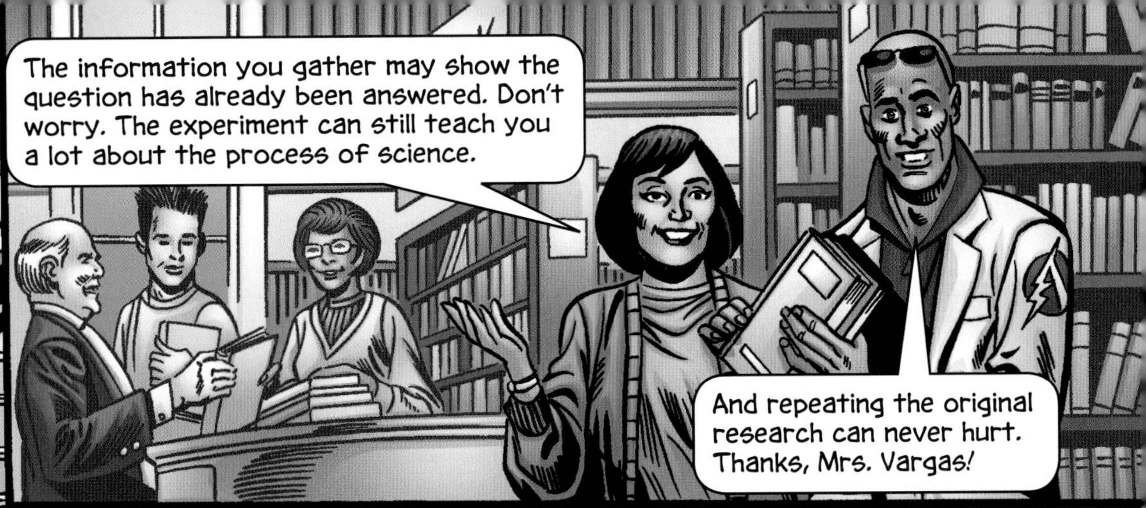
The information you gather may show the question has already been answered. Don't worry. The experiment can still teach you a lot about the process of science.
And repeating the original research can never hurt. Thanks, Mrs. Vargas!

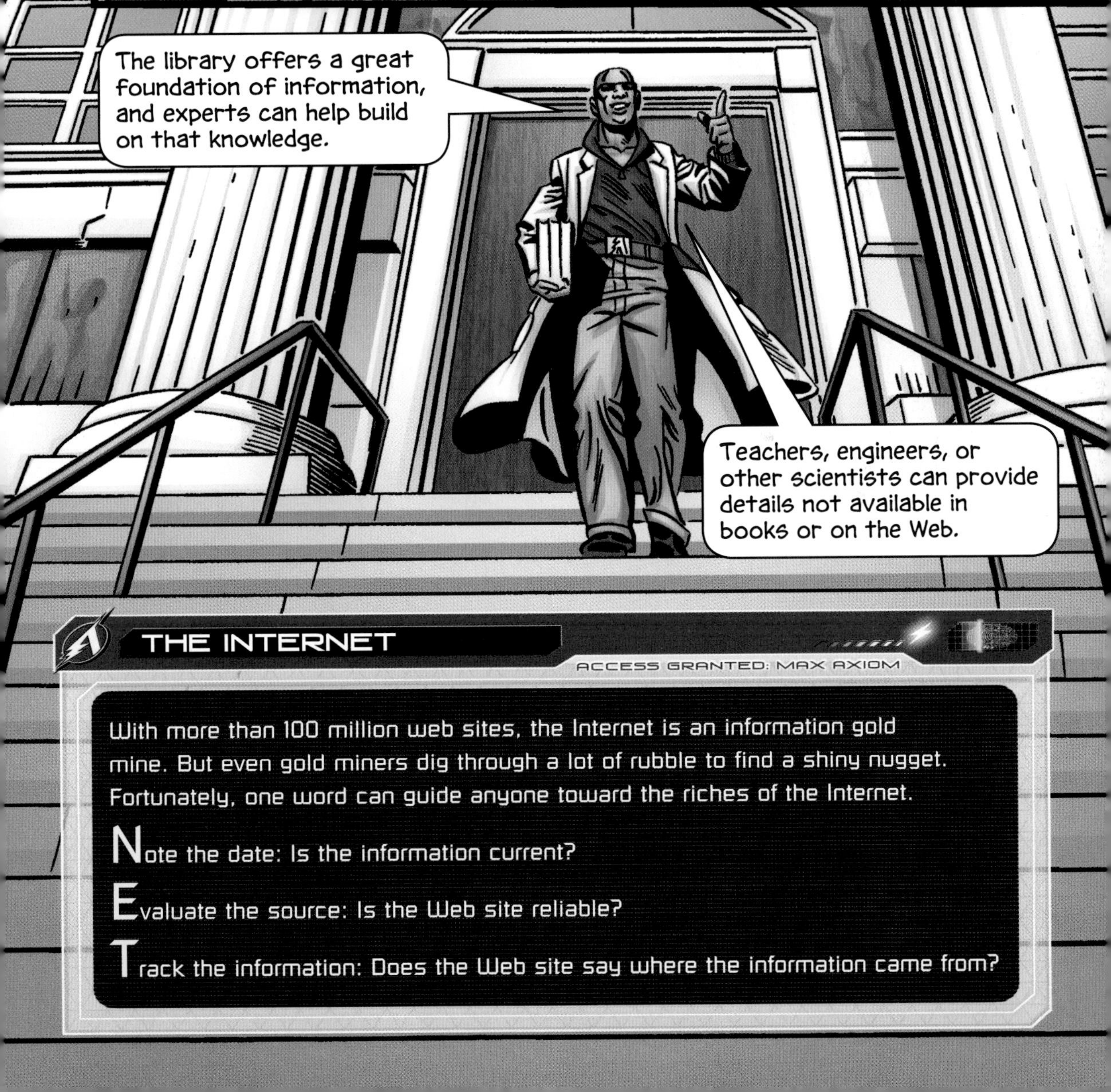
The library offers a great foundation of information, and experts can help build on that knowledge.
Teachers, engineers, or other scientists can provide details not available in books or on the Web.

## THE INTERNET

ACCESS GRANTED: MAX AXIOM

With more than 100 million web sites, the Internet is an information gold mine. But even gold miners dig through a lot of rubble to find a shiny nugget. Fortunately, one word can guide anyone toward the riches of the Internet.

**N**ote the date: Is the information current?

**E**valuate the source: Is the Web site reliable?

**T**rack the information: Does the Web site say where the information came from?

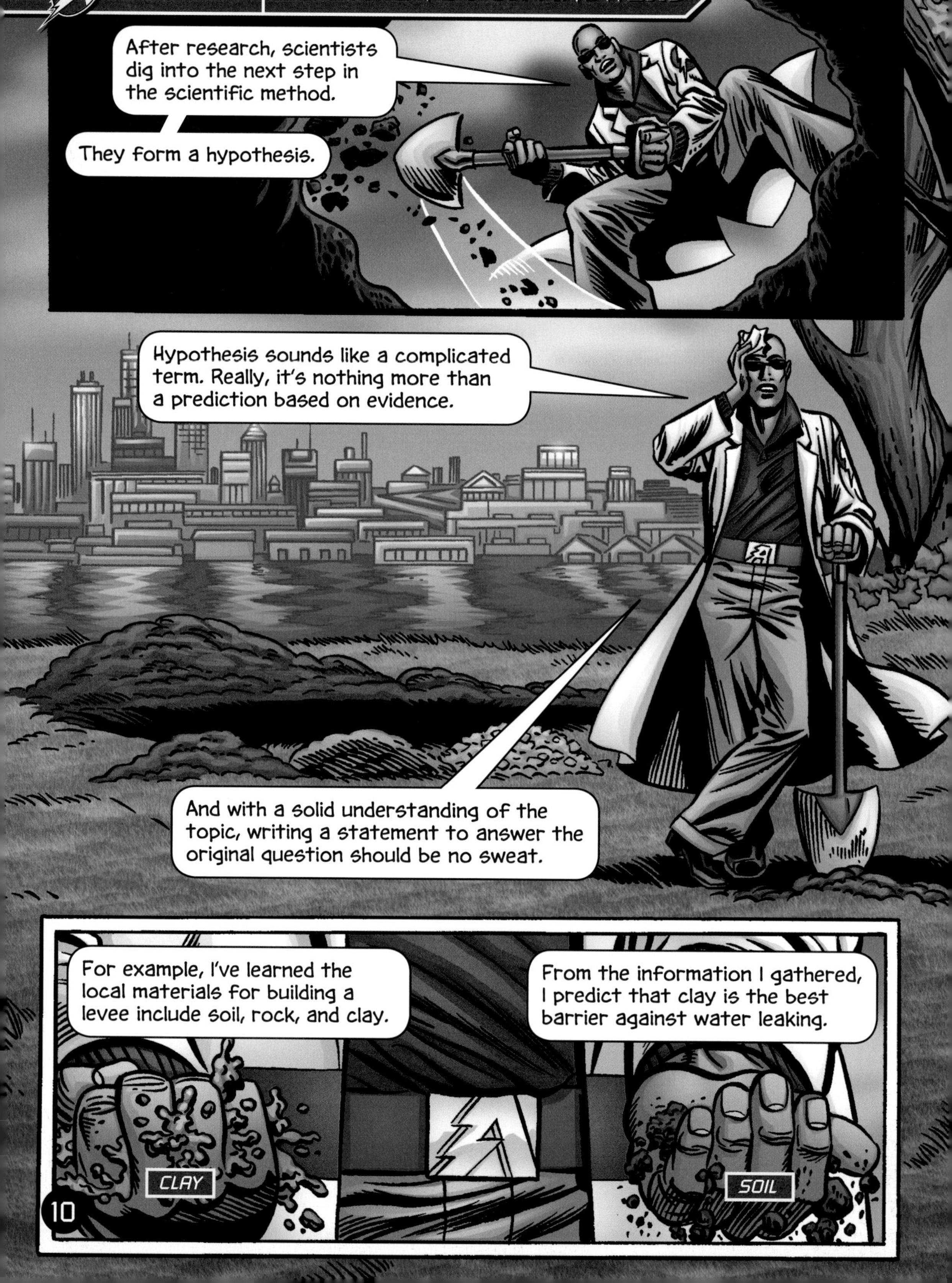
After research, scientists dig into the next step in the scientific method.
They form a hypothesis.
Hypothesis sounds like a complicated term. Really, it's nothing more than a prediction based on evidence.
And with a solid understanding of the topic, writing a statement to answer the original question should be no sweat.
For example, I've learned the local materials for building a levee include soil, rock, and clay.
From the information I gathered, I predict that clay is the best barrier against water leaking.
CLAY
SOIL

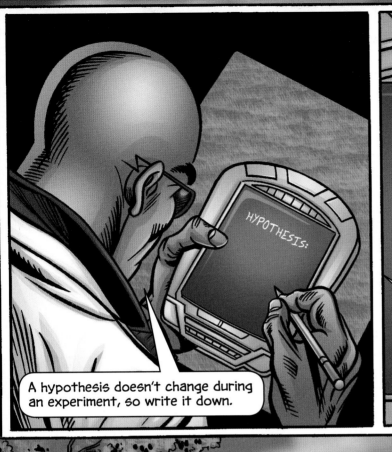

HYPOTHESIS:

HYPOTHESIS: Clay will hold back more water than soil or rock.

This record helps maintain a clear direction during the project.

A hypothesis doesn't change during an experiment, so write it down.

And don't worry about the hypothesis being correct. The main purpose of an experiment is to show whether the data you collect supports the hypothesis.

With a solid question, information, and hypothesis, the experiment is about to really take off.

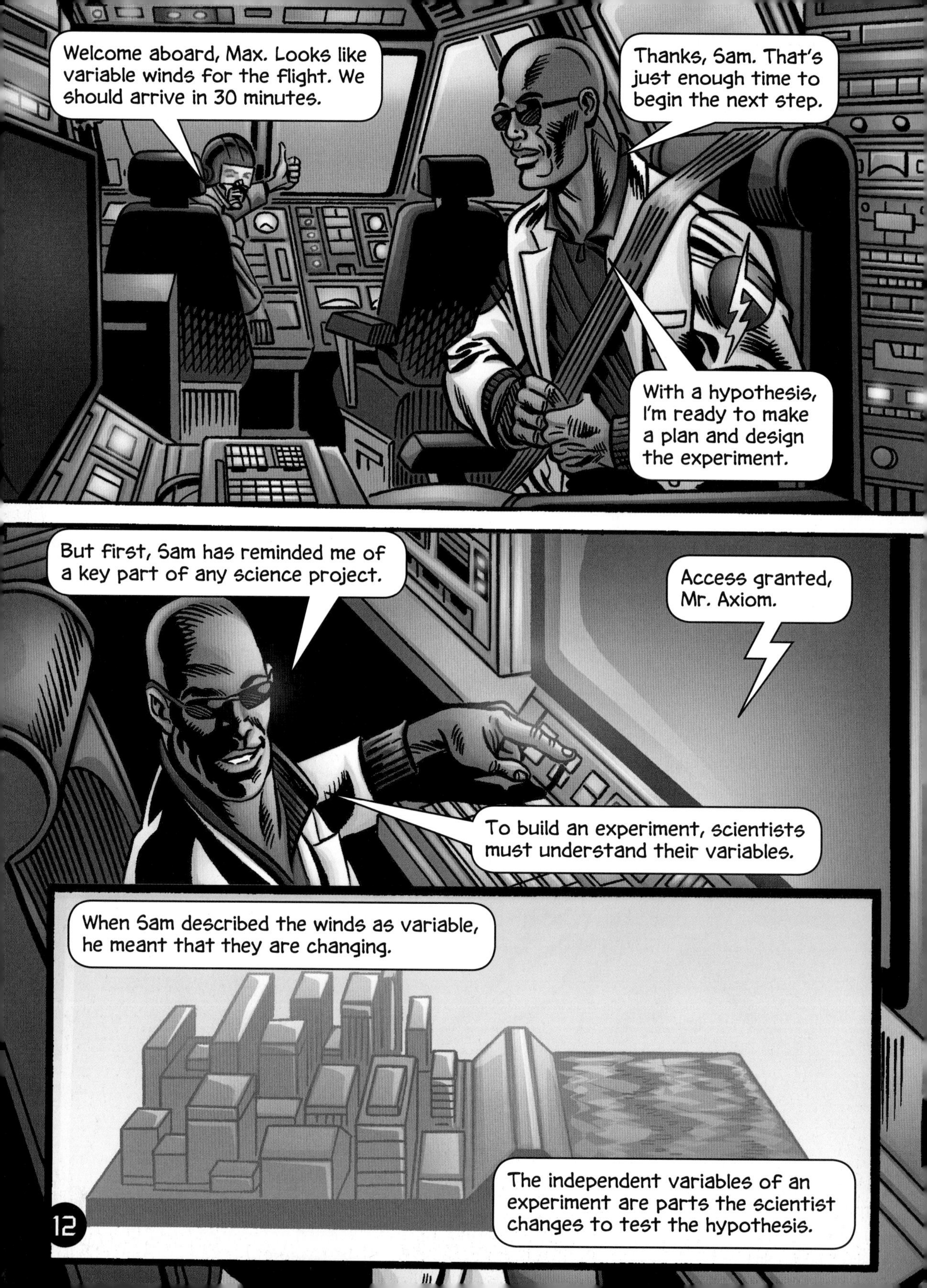
Welcome aboard, Max. Looks like variable winds for the flight. We should arrive in 30 minutes.
Thanks, Sam. That's just enough time to begin the next step.
With a hypothesis, I'm ready to make a plan and design the experiment.
But first, Sam has reminded me of a key part of any science project.
Access granted, Mr. Axiom.
To build an experiment, scientists must understand their variables.
When Sam described the winds as variable, he meant that they are changing.
The independent variables of an experiment are parts the scientist changes to test the hypothesis.

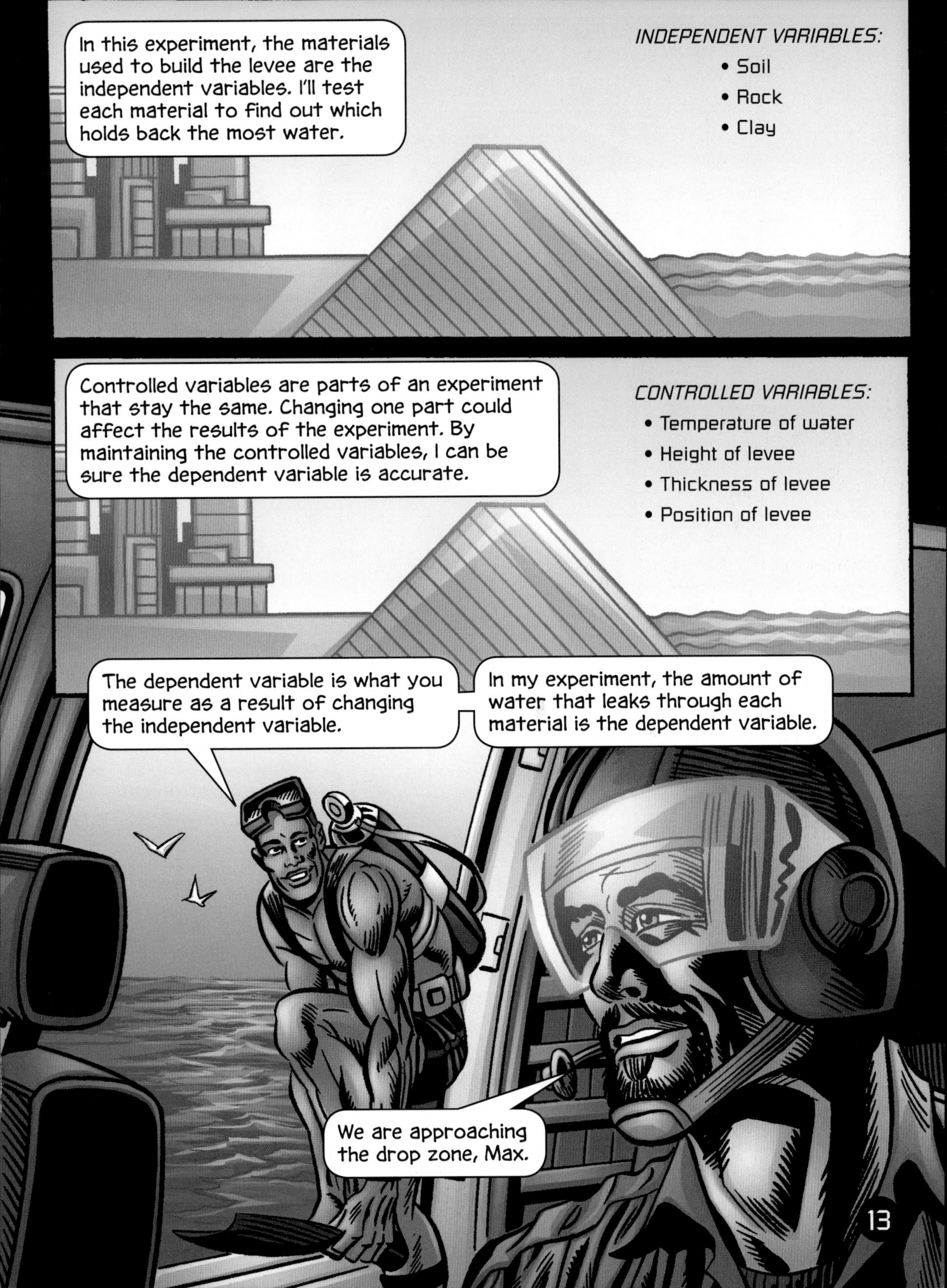
In this experiment, the materials used to build the levee are the independent variables. I'll test each material to find out which holds back the most water.
INDEPENDENT VARIABLES:
• Soil
• Rock
• Clay
Controlled variables are parts of an experiment that stay the same. Changing one part could affect the results of the experiment. By maintaining the controlled variables, I can be sure the dependent variable is accurate.
CONTROLLED VARIABLES:
• Temperature of water
• Height of levee
• Thickness of levee
• Position of levee
The dependent variable is what you measure as a result of changing the independent variable.
In my experiment, the amount of water that leaks through each material is the dependent variable.
We are approaching the drop zone, Max.

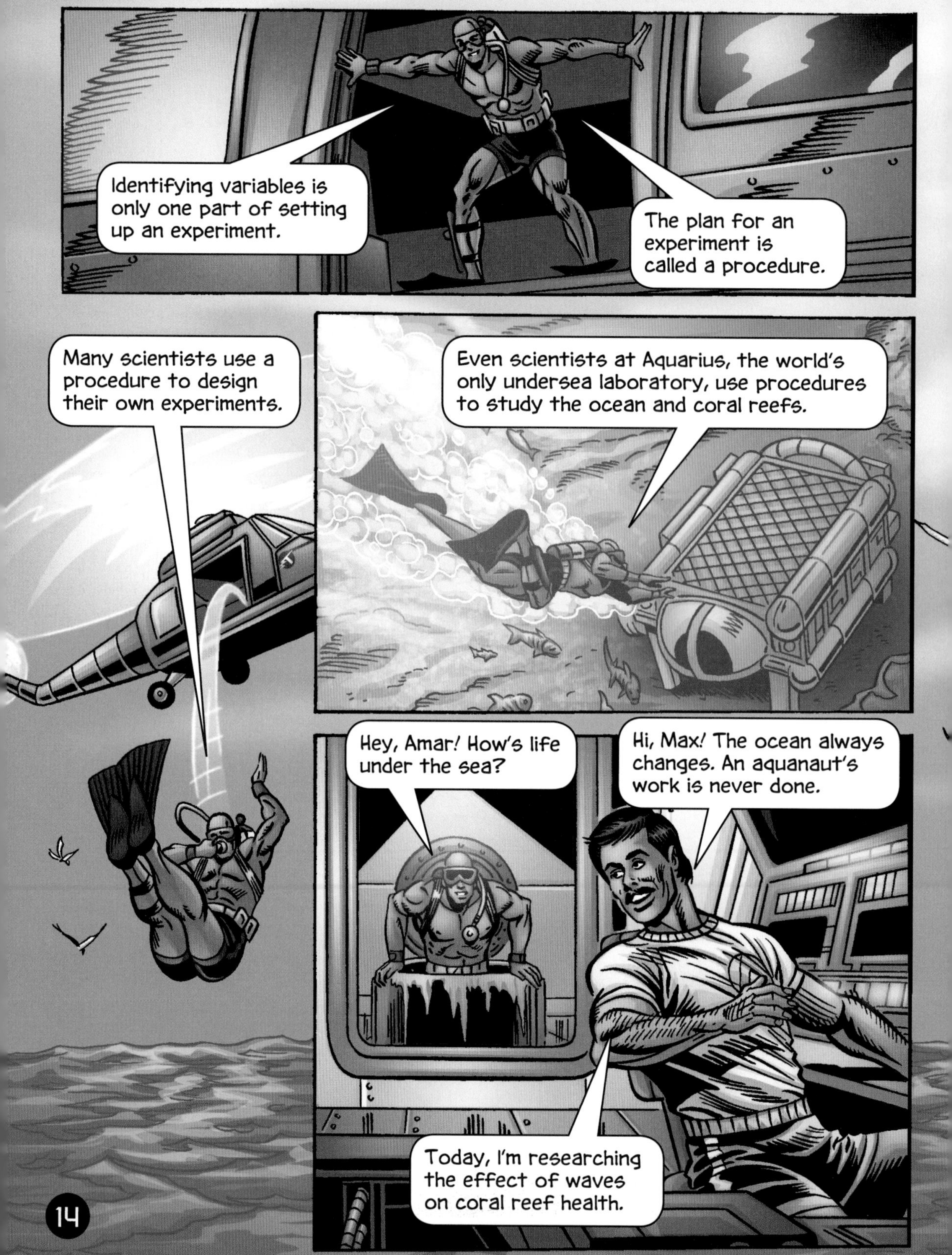
Identifying variables is only one part of setting up an experiment.
The plan for an experiment is called a procedure.
Many scientists use a procedure to design their own experiments.
Even scientists at Aquarius, the world's only undersea laboratory, use procedures to study the ocean and coral reefs.
Hey, Amar! How's life under the sea?
Hi, Max! The ocean always changes. An aquanaut's work is never done.
Today, I'm researching the effect of waves on coral reef health.

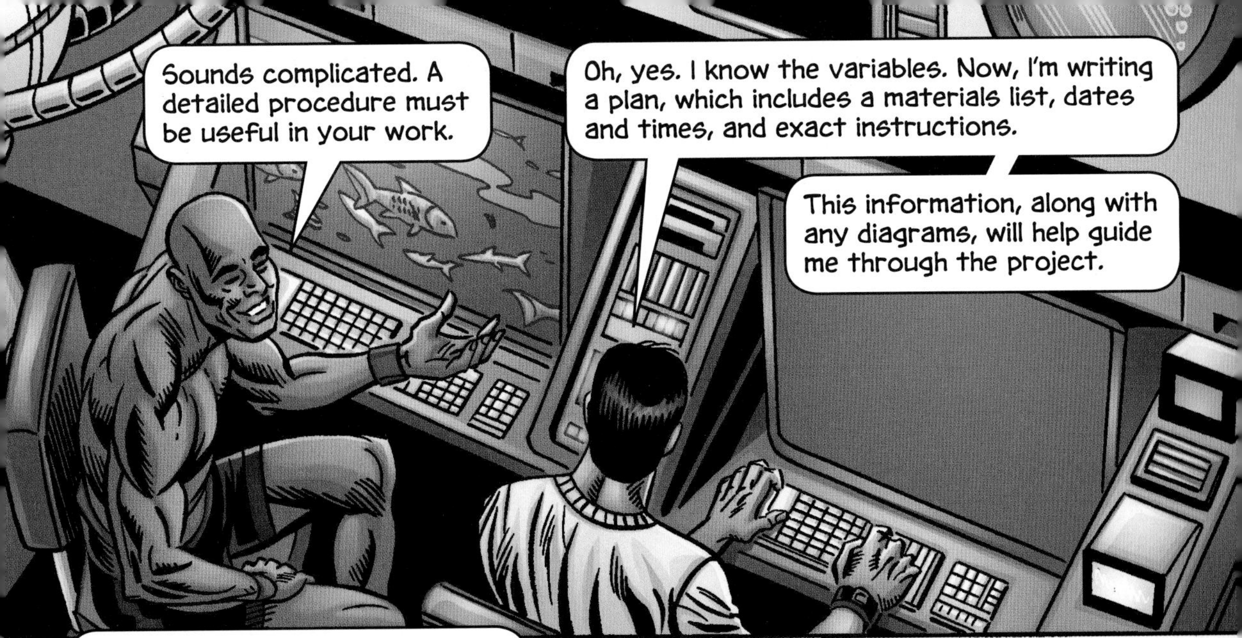
Sounds complicated. A detailed procedure must be useful in your work.
Oh, yes. I know the variables. Now, I'm writing a plan, which includes a materials list, dates and times, and exact instructions.
This information, along with any diagrams, will help guide me through the project.

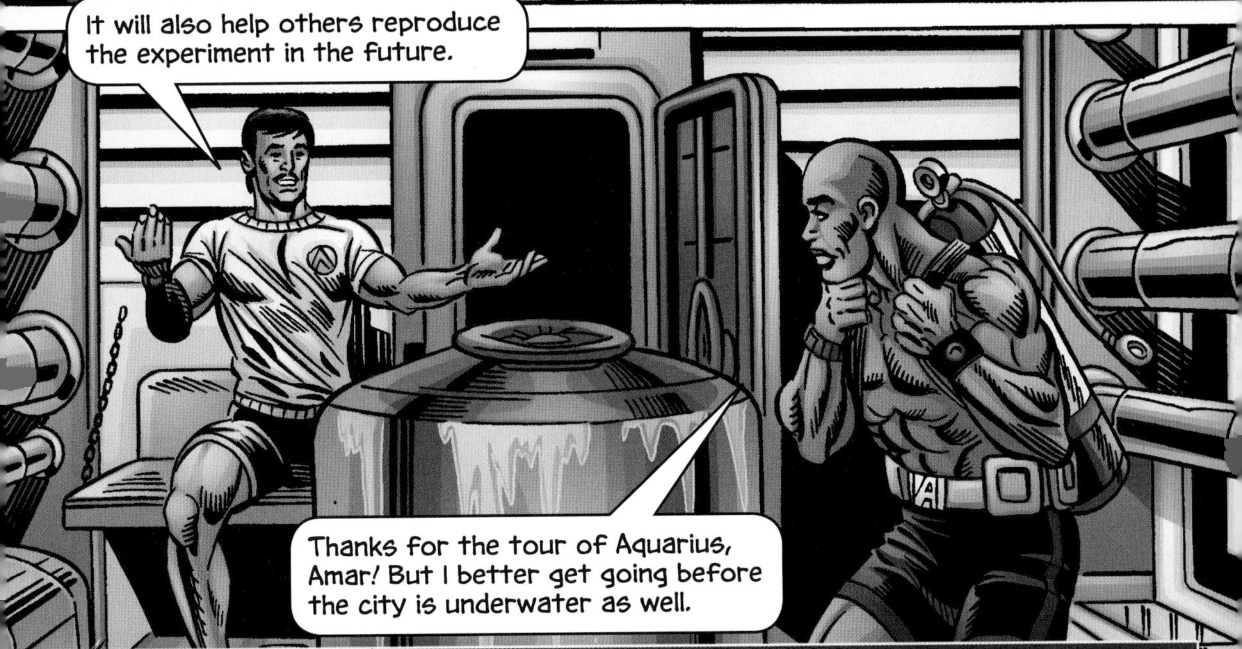
It will also help others reproduce the experiment in the future.
Thanks for the tour of Aquarius, Amar! But I better get going before the city is underwater as well.

## MORE ABOUT *AQUARIUS*

ACCESS GRANTED: MAX AXIOM

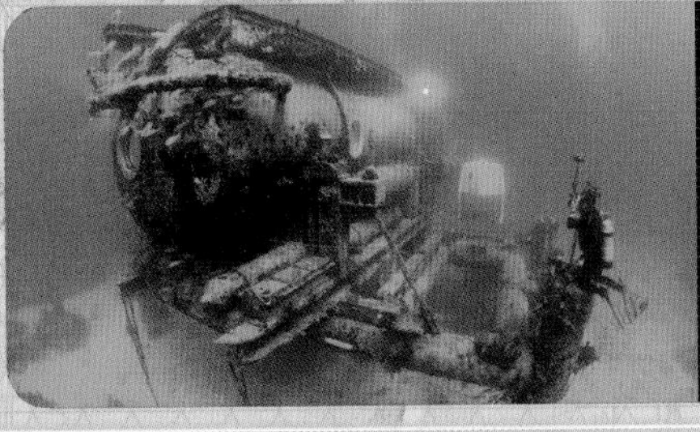

*Aquarius* is located 63 feet (19 meters) beneath the ocean surface in the Florida Keys National Marine Sanctuary. *Aquarius* allows scientists to stay underwater for an extended period of time. The extra time allows longer research, including coral reef monitoring and NASA equipment testing.

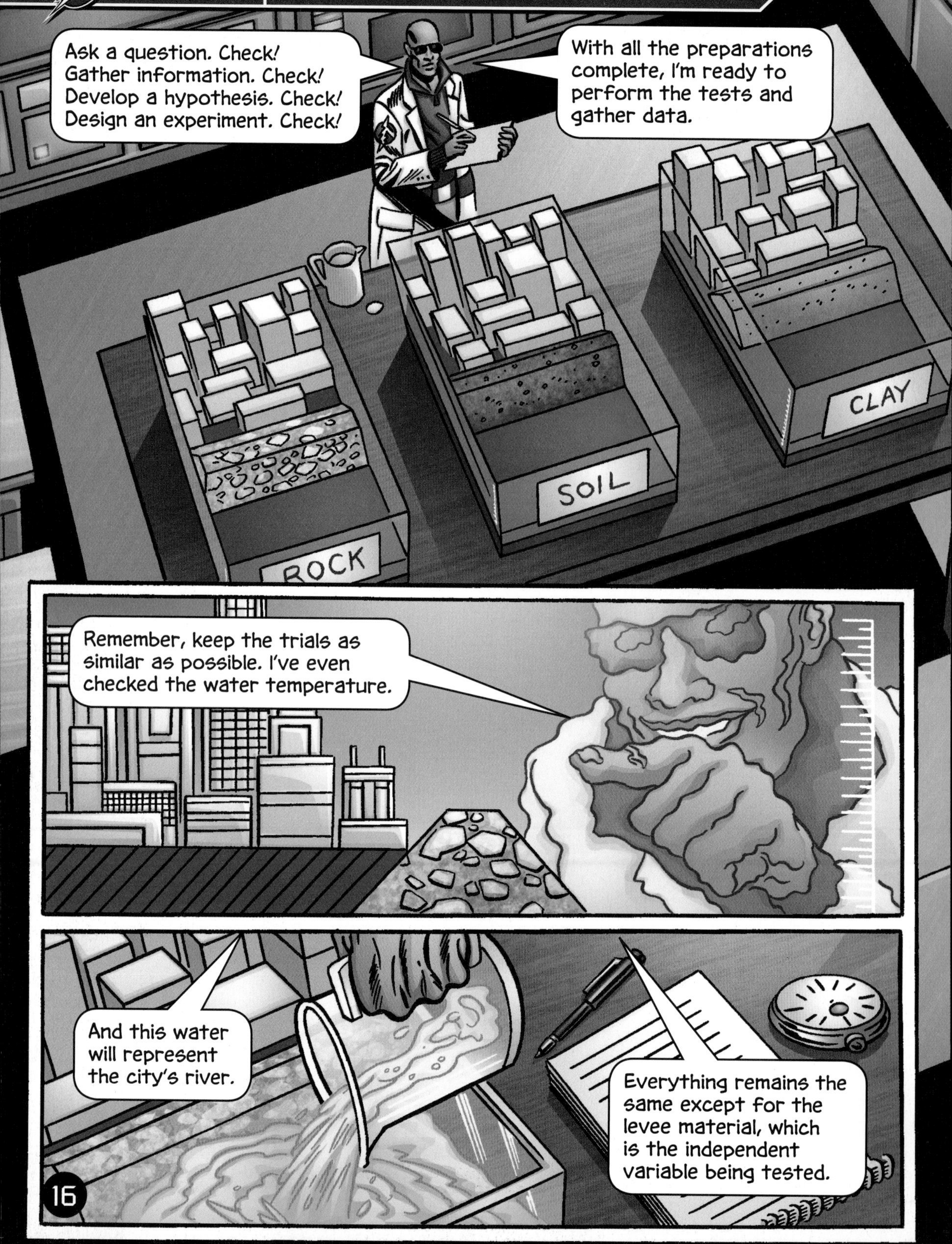
Ask a question. Check! Gather information. Check! Develop a hypothesis. Check! Design an experiment. Check!
With all the preparations complete, I'm ready to perform the tests and gather data.
ROCK
SOIL
CLAY
Remember, keep the trials as similar as possible. I've even checked the water temperature.
And this water will represent the city's river.
Everything remains the same except for the levee material, which is the independent variable being tested.

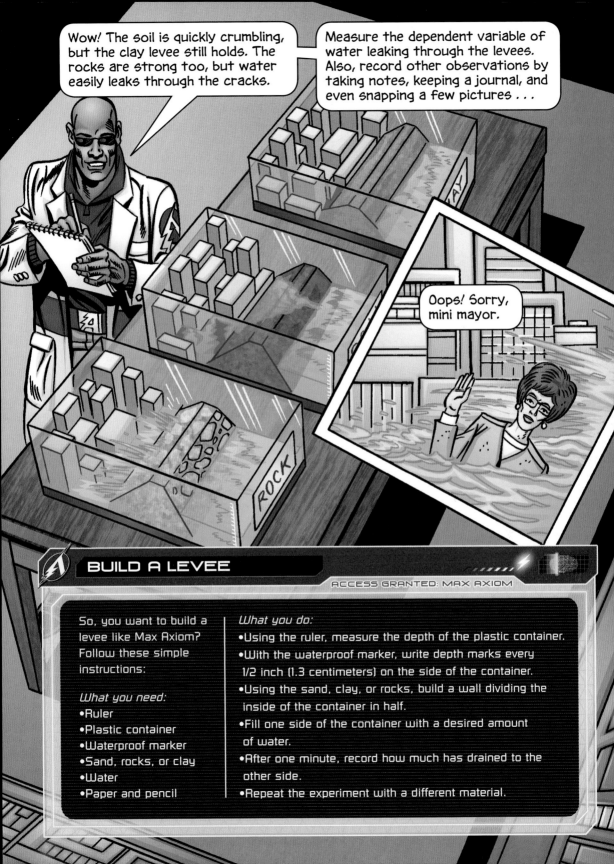

Wow! The soil is quickly crumbling, but the clay levee still holds. The rocks are strong too, but water easily leaks through the cracks.

Measure the dependent variable of water leaking through the levees. Also, record other observations by taking notes, keeping a journal, and even snapping a few pictures . . .

Oops! Sorry, mini mayor.

# BUILD A LEVEE

ACCESS GRANTED: MAX AXIOM

So, you want to build a levee like Max Axiom? Follow these simple instructions:

*What you need:*
•Ruler
•Plastic container
•Waterproof marker
•Sand, rocks, or clay
•Water
•Paper and pencil

*What you do:*
•Using the ruler, measure the depth of the plastic container.
•With the waterproof marker, write depth marks every 1/2 inch (1.3 centimeters) on the side of the container.
•Using the sand, clay, or rocks, build a wall dividing the inside of the container in half.
•Fill one side of the container with a desired amount of water.
•After one minute, record how much has drained to the other side.
•Repeat the experiment with a different material.

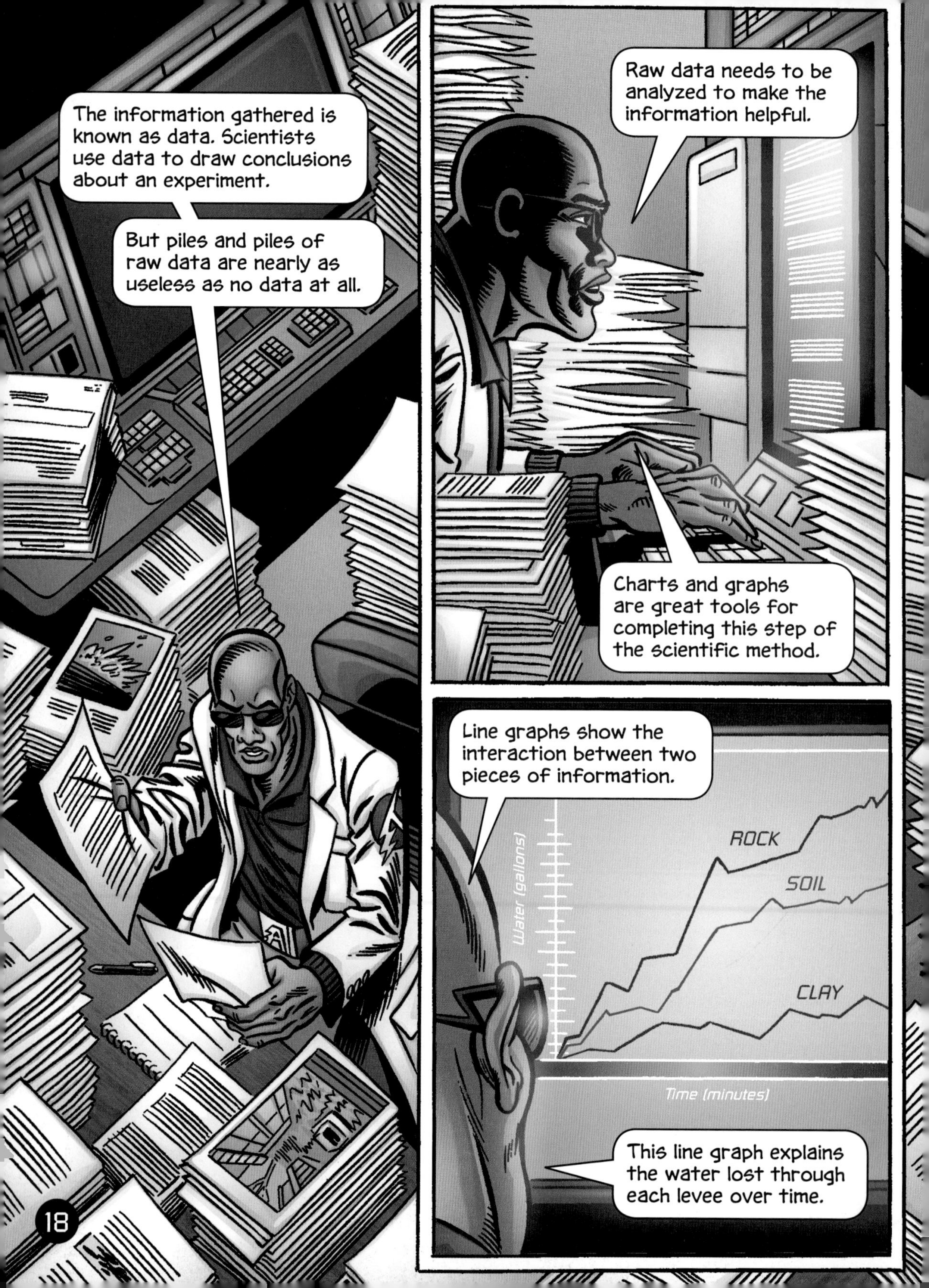
The information gathered is known as data. Scientists use data to draw conclusions about an experiment.
But piles and piles of raw data are nearly as useless as no data at all.
Raw data needs to be analyzed to make the information helpful.
Charts and graphs are great tools for completing this step of the scientific method.
Line graphs show the interaction between two pieces of information.
Water (gallons)
ROCK
SOIL
CLAY
Time (minutes)
This line graph explains the water lost through each levee over time.

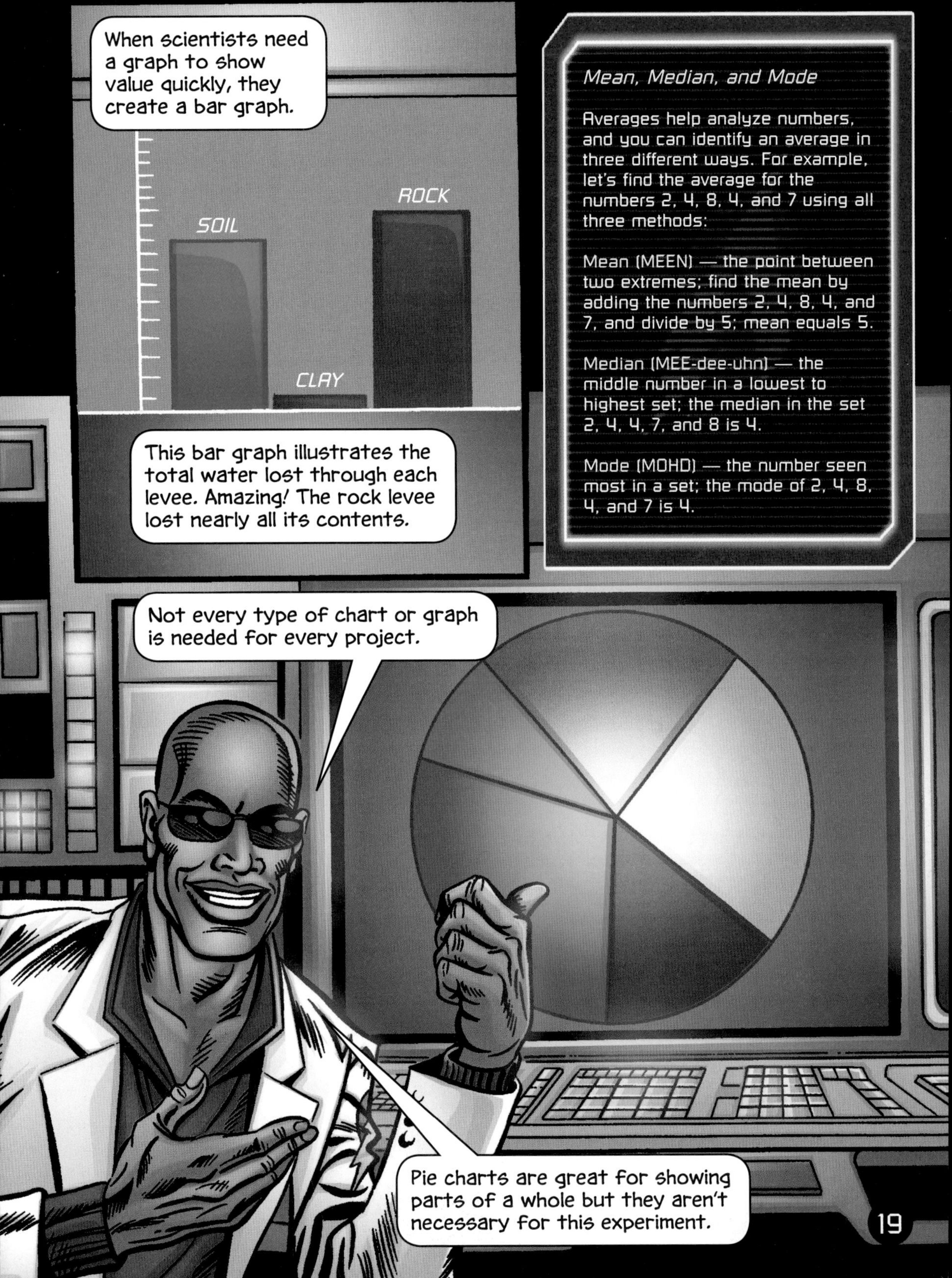
When scientists need a graph to show value quickly, they create a bar graph.
SOIL
ROCK
CLAY
This bar graph illustrates the total water lost through each levee. Amazing! The rock levee lost nearly all its contents.
Mean, Median, and Mode
Averages help analyze numbers, and you can identify an average in three different ways. For example, let's find the average for the numbers 2, 4, 8, 4, and 7 using all three methods:
Mean (MEEN) — the point between two extremes; find the mean by adding the numbers 2, 4, 8, 4, and 7, and divide by 5; mean equals 5.
Median (MEE-dee-uhn) — the middle number in a lowest to highest set; the median in the set 2, 4, 4, 7, and 8 is 4.
Mode (MOHD) — the number seen most in a set; the mode of 2, 4, 8, 4, and 7 is 4.
Not every type of chart or graph is needed for every project.
Pie charts are great for showing parts of a whole but they aren't necessary for this experiment.

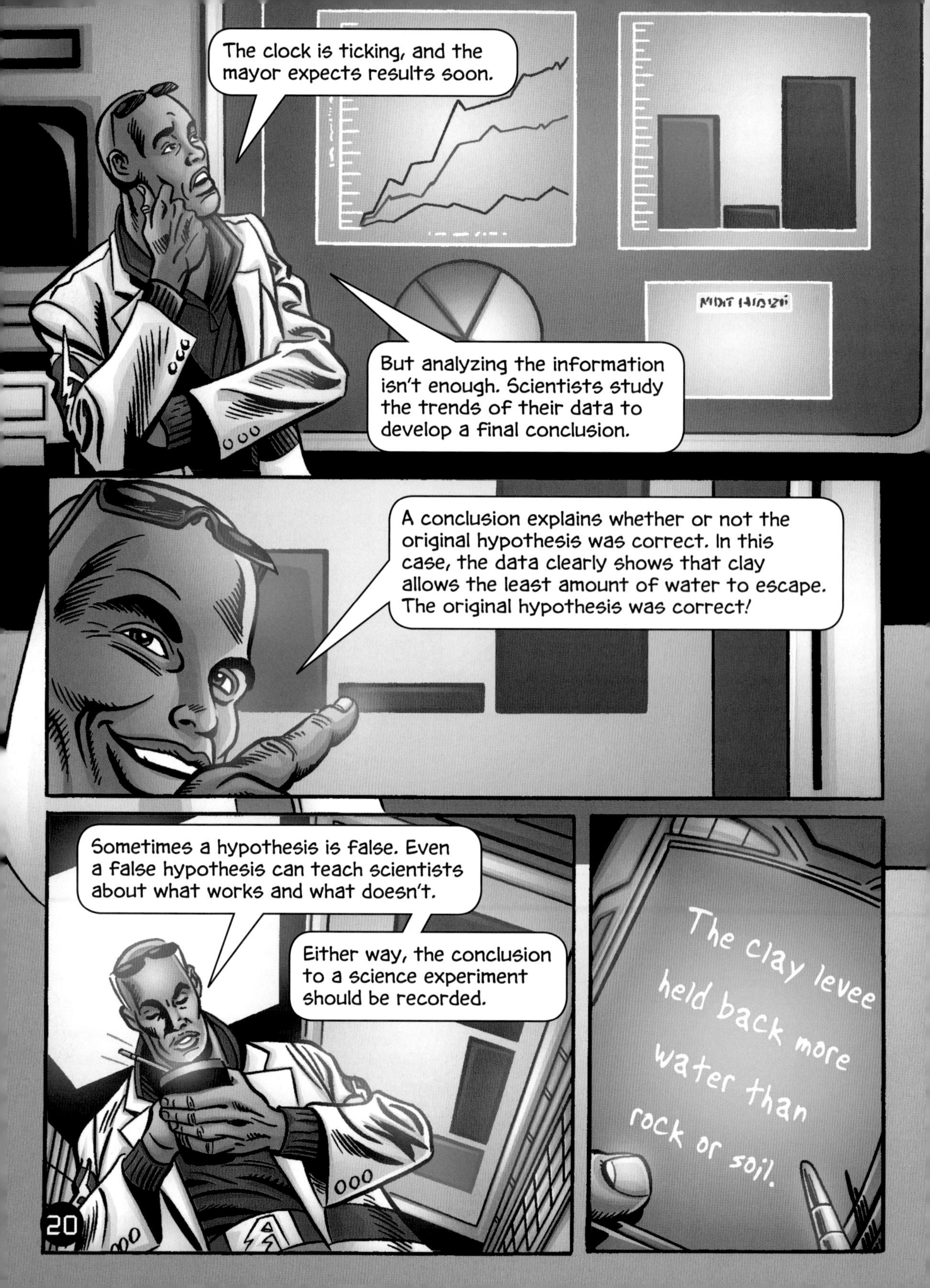

The clock is ticking, and the mayor expects results soon.
But analyzing the information isn't enough. Scientists study the trends of their data to develop a final conclusion.
A conclusion explains whether or not the original hypothesis was correct. In this case, the data clearly shows that clay allows the least amount of water to escape. The original hypothesis was correct!
Sometimes a hypothesis is false. Even a false hypothesis can teach scientists about what works and what doesn't.
Either way, the conclusion to a science experiment should be recorded.
The clay levee held back more water than rock or soil.

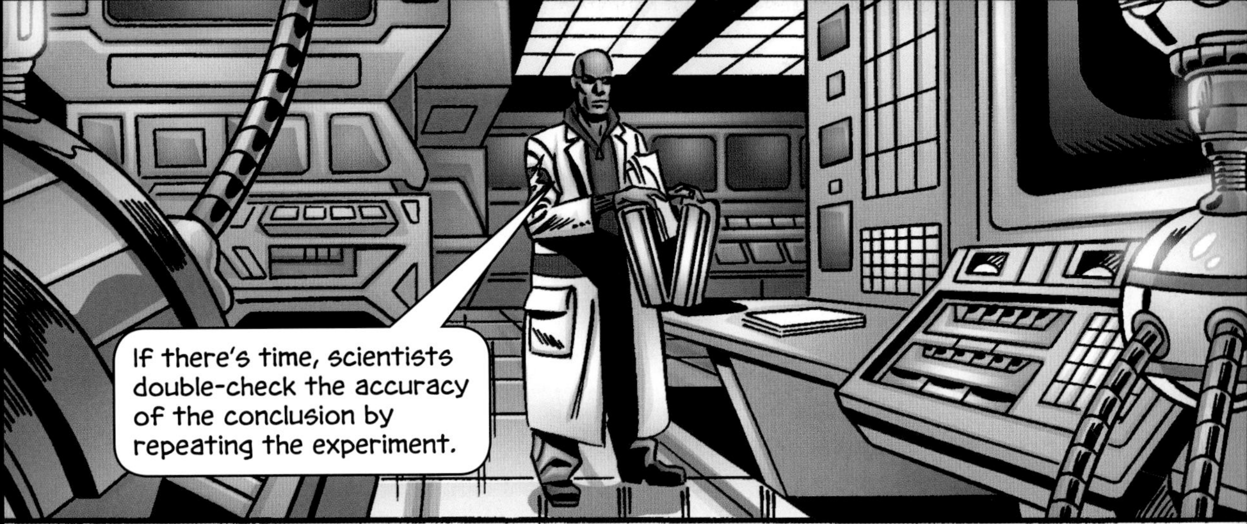
If there's time, scientists double-check the accuracy of the conclusion by repeating the experiment.

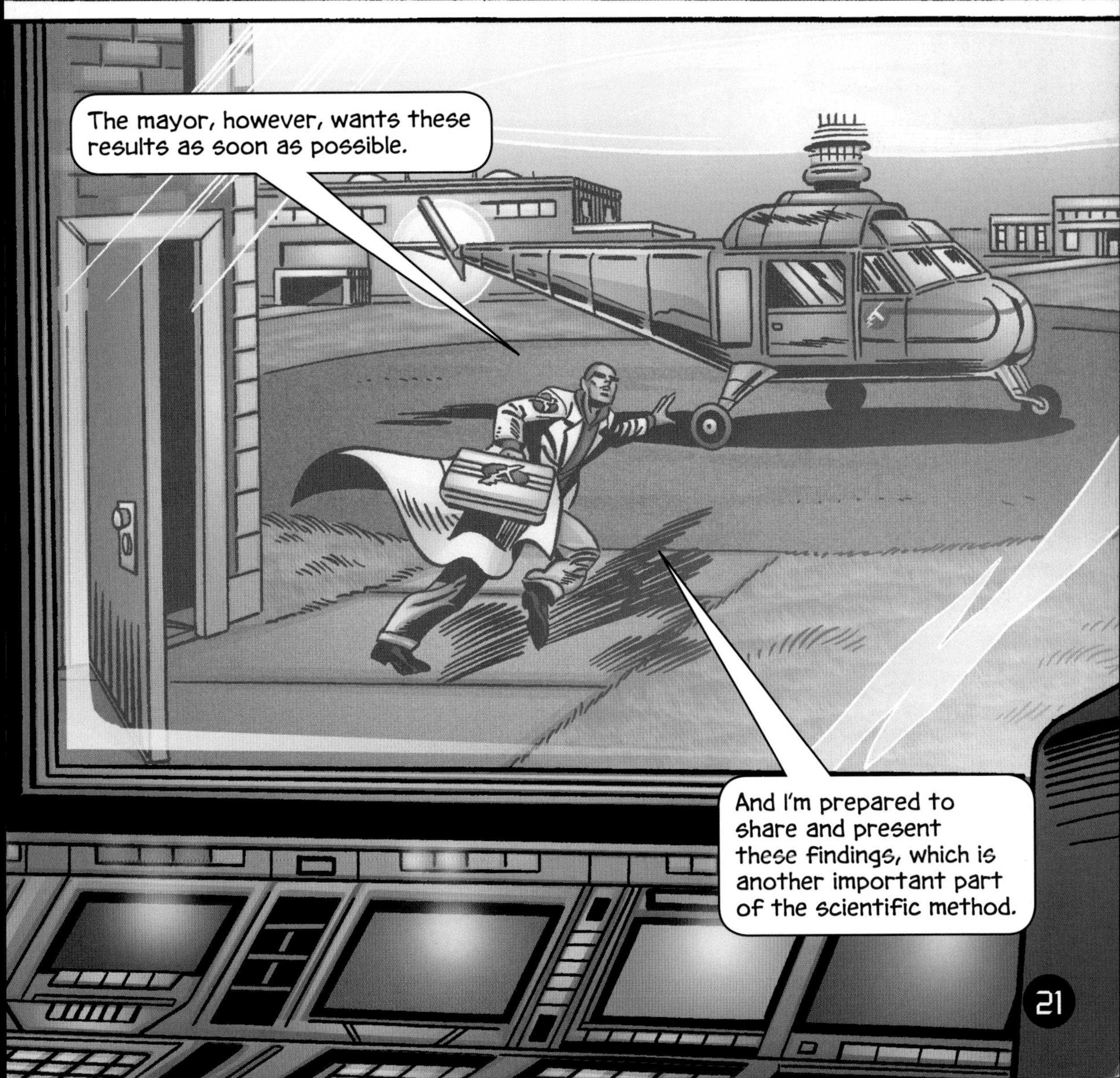
The mayor, however, wants these results as soon as possible.
And I'm prepared to share and present these findings, which is another important part of the scientific method.

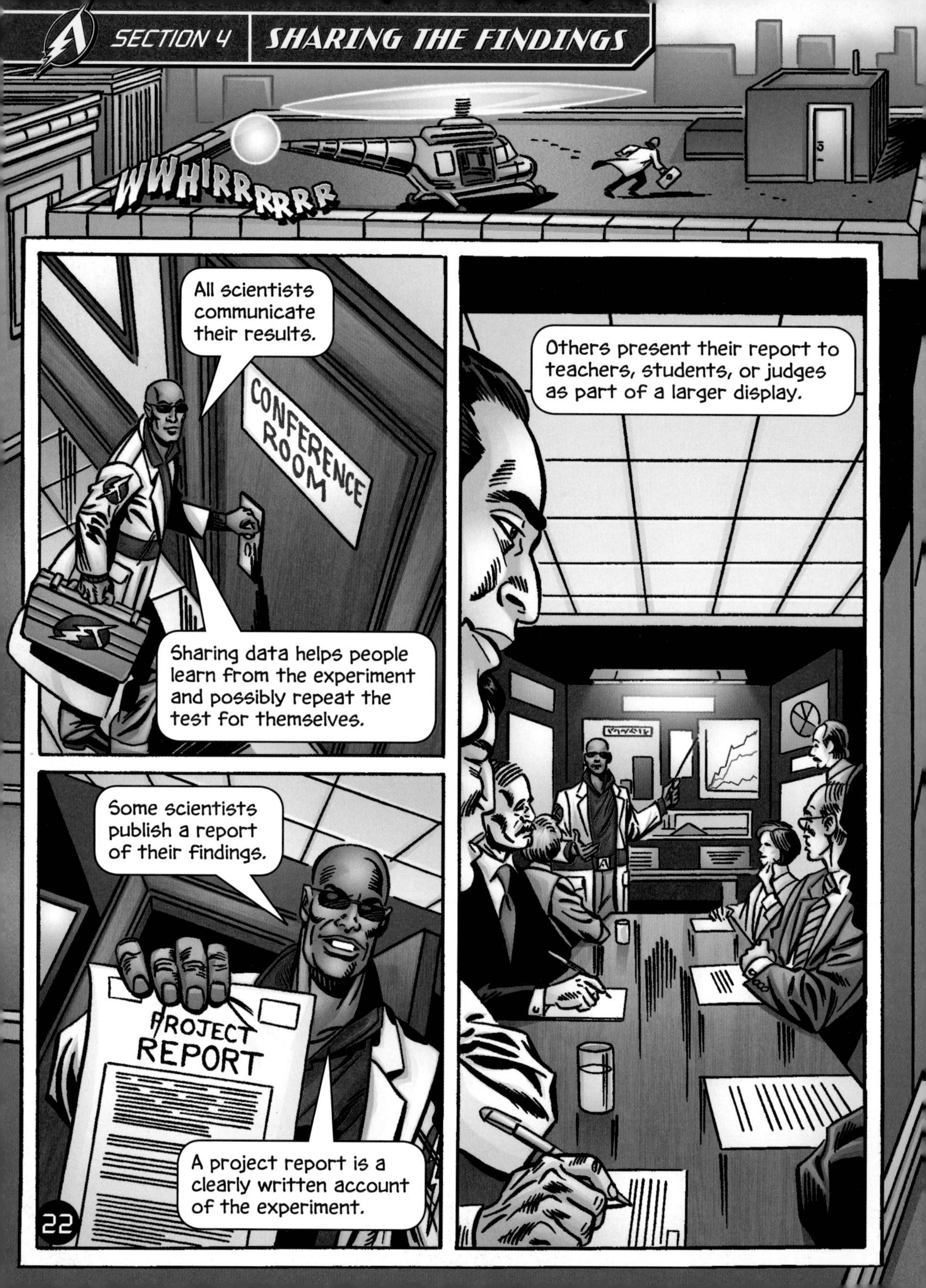

SECTION 4
SHARING THE FINDINGS
WWHIRRRRRRR
All scientists communicate their results.
CONFERENCE ROOM
Sharing data helps people learn from the experiment and possibly repeat the test for themselves.
Some scientists publish a report of their findings.
PROJECT REPORT
A project report is a clearly written account of the experiment.
Others present their report to teachers, students, or judges as part of a larger display.

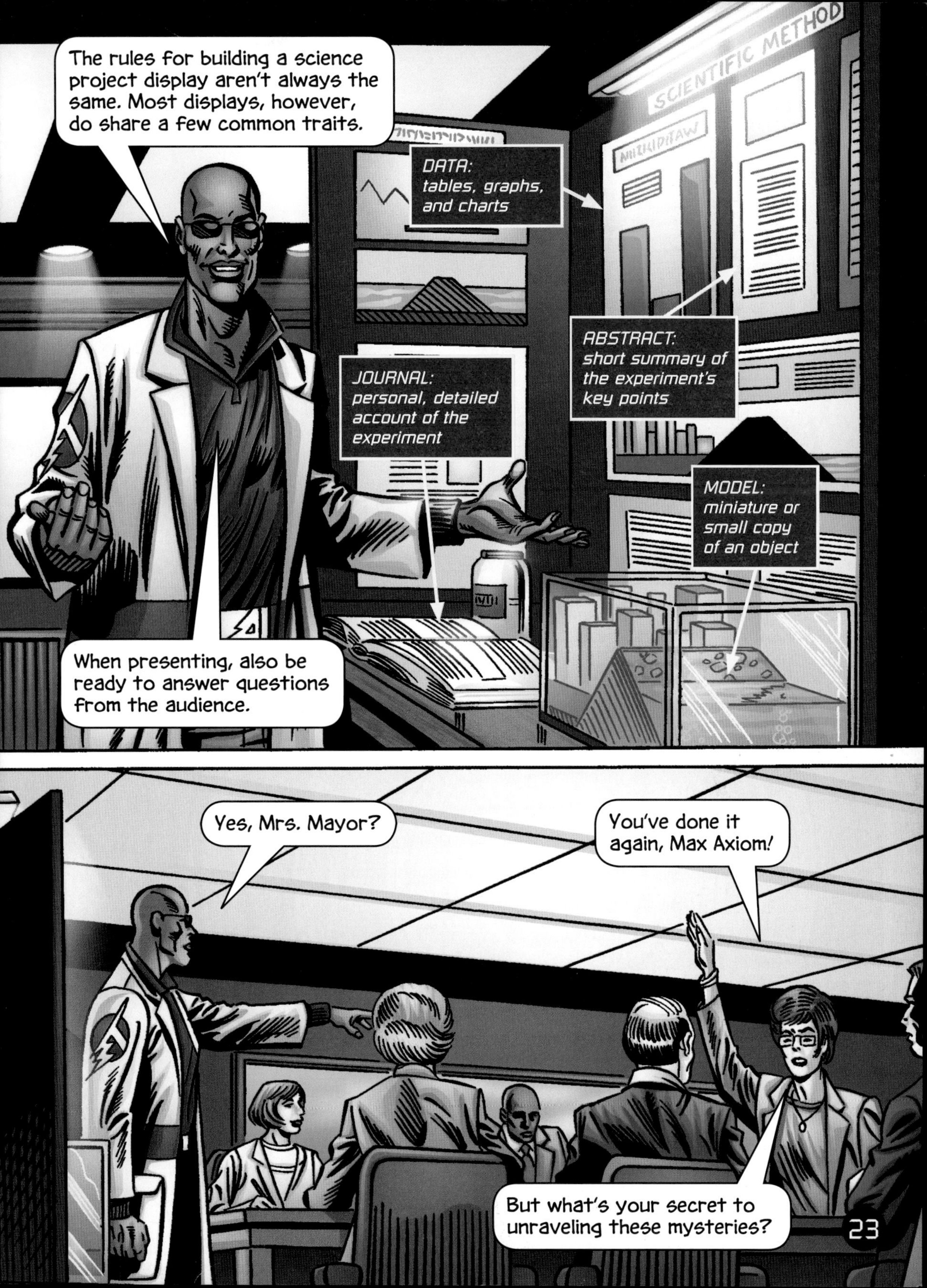

The rules for building a science project display aren't always the same. Most displays, however, do share a few common traits.
SCIENTIFIC METHOD
DATA: tables, graphs, and charts
ABSTRACT: short summary of the experiment's key points
JOURNAL: personal, detailed account of the experiment
MODEL: miniature or small copy of an object
When presenting, also be ready to answer questions from the audience.
Yes, Mrs. Mayor?
You've done it again, Max Axiom!
But what's your secret to unraveling these mysteries?

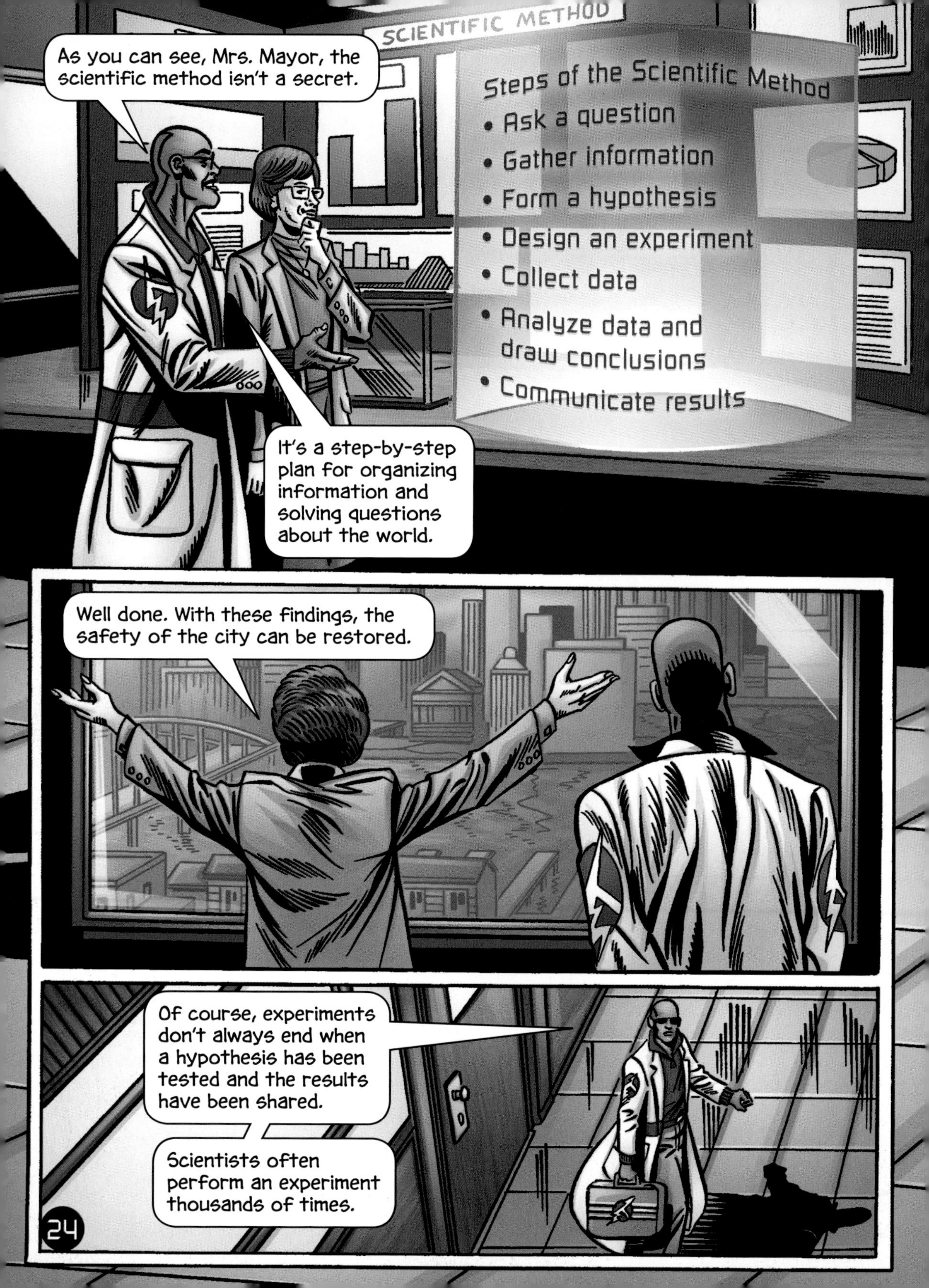
SCIENTIFIC METHOD
As you can see, Mrs. Mayor, the scientific method isn't a secret.
Steps of the Scientific Method
• Ask a question
• Gather information
• Form a hypothesis
• Design an experiment
• Collect data
• Analyze data and draw conclusions
• Communicate results
It's a step-by-step plan for organizing information and solving questions about the world.
Well done. With these findings, the safety of the city can be restored.
Of course, experiments don't always end when a hypothesis has been tested and the results have been shared.
Scientists often perform an experiment thousands of times.

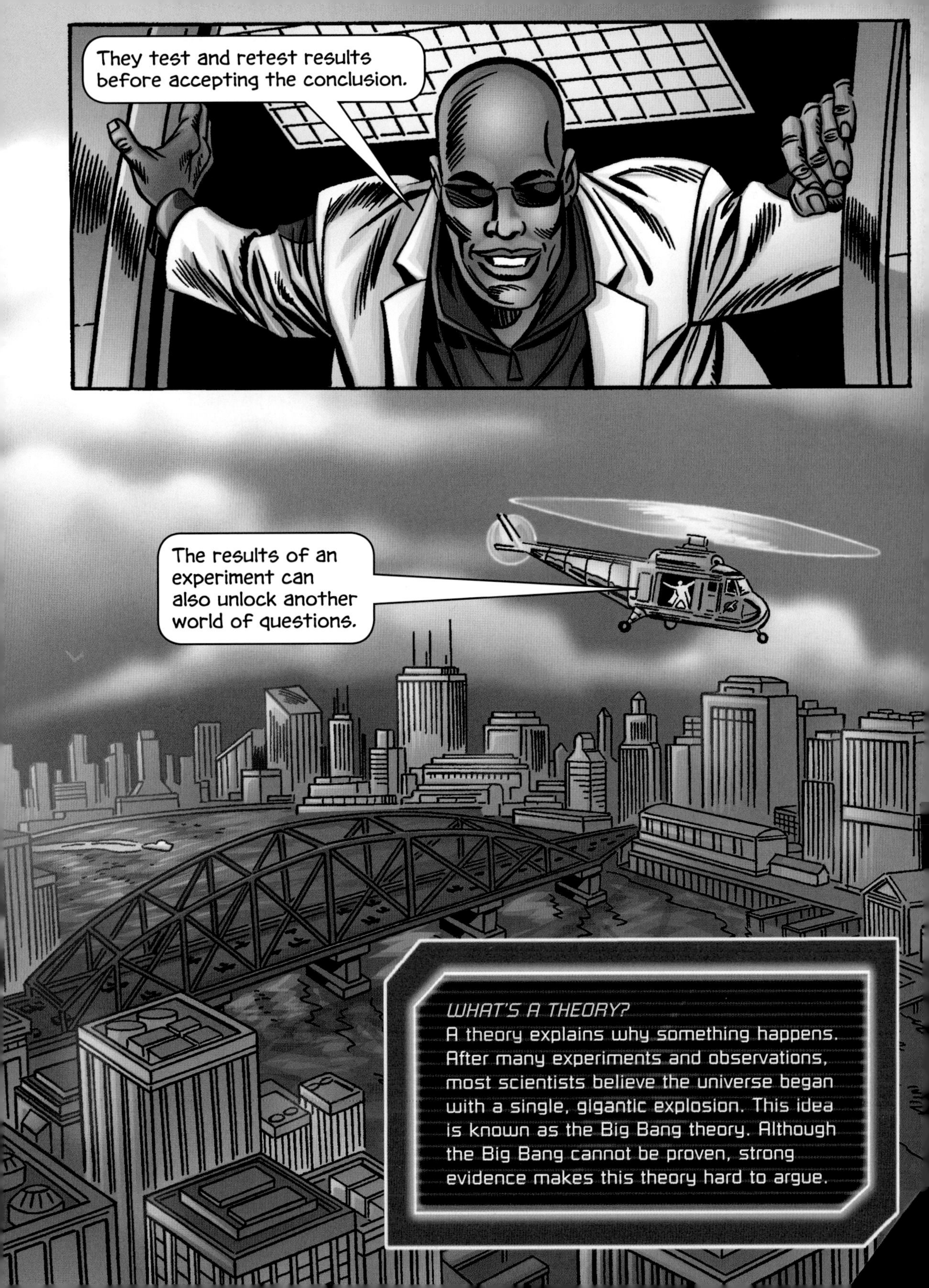
They test and retest results before accepting the conclusion.
The results of an experiment can also unlock another world of questions.

*WHAT'S A THEORY?*

A theory explains why something happens. After many experiments and observations, most scientists believe the universe began with a single, gigantic explosion. This idea is known as the Big Bang theory. Although the Big Bang cannot be proven, strong evidence makes this theory hard to argue.

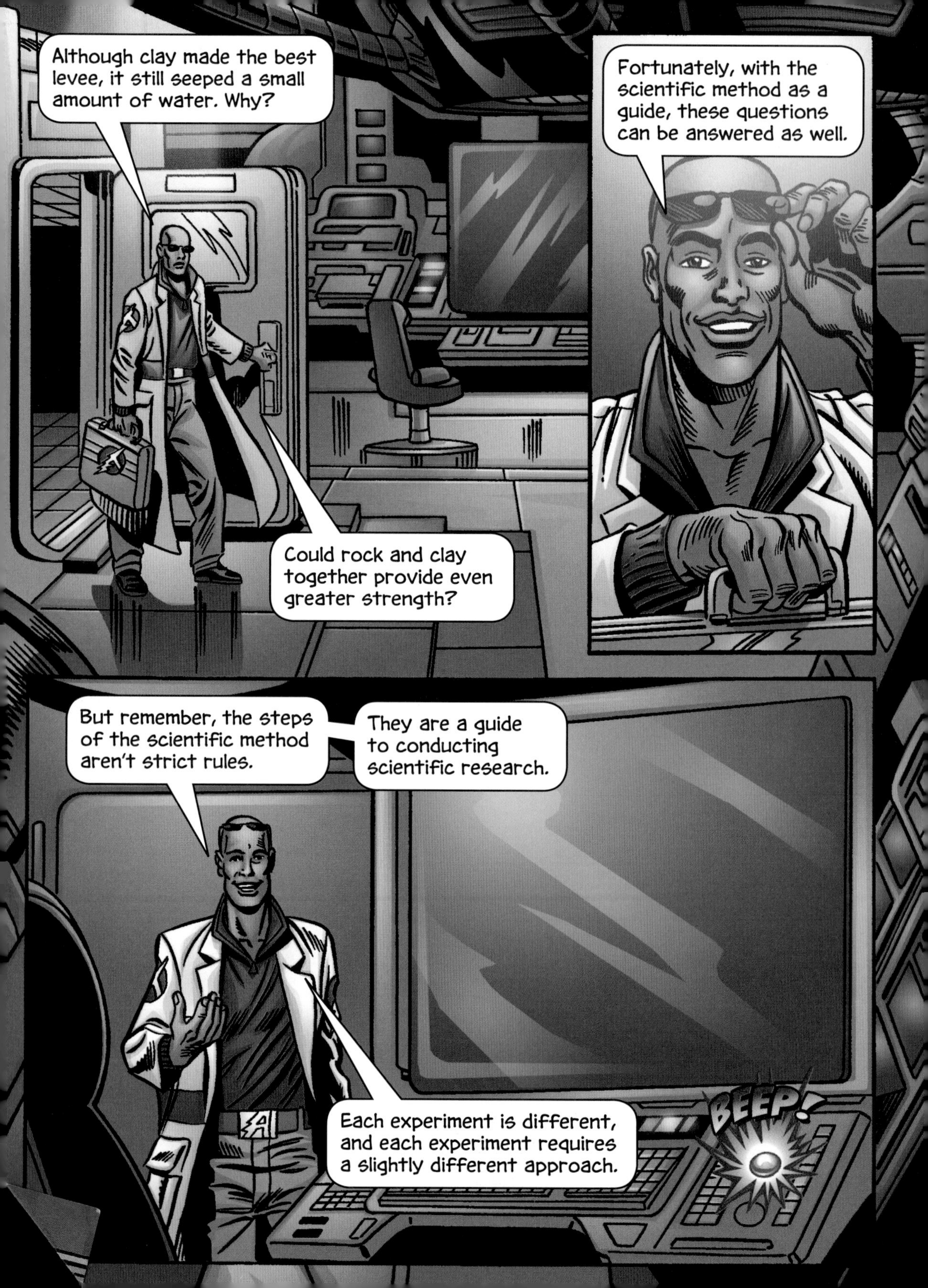

Although clay made the best levee, it still seeped a small amount of water. Why?
Could rock and clay together provide even greater strength?
Fortunately, with the scientific method as a guide, these questions can be answered as well.
But remember, the steps of the scientific method aren't strict rules.
They are a guide to conducting scientific research.
Each experiment is different, and each experiment requires a slightly different approach.
BEEP!

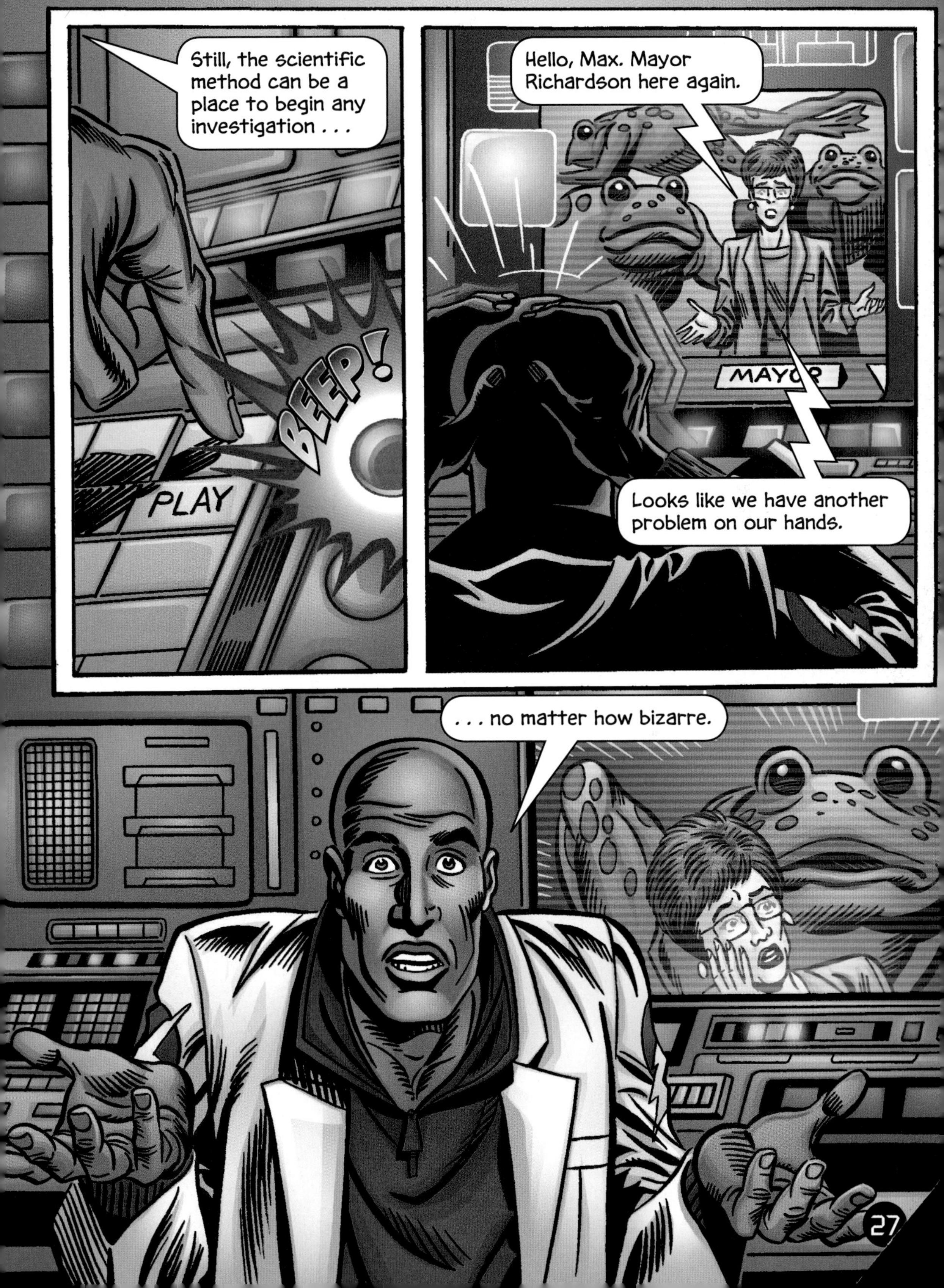
Still, the scientific method can be a place to begin any investigation . . .
BEEP!
PLAY
Hello, Max. Mayor Richardson here again.
MAYOR
Looks like we have another problem on our hands.
. . . no matter how bizarre.

# MORE ABOUT THE SCIENTIFIC METHOD

 Throughout history, people have answered questions by observing and recording data. No one knows who developed the scientific method. Still, many believe Francesco Redi, an Italian physician, performed the first experiment to match this step-by-step plan. In 1668, most scientists believed maggots grew directly from rotten meat. Redi, however, believed maggots hatched from fly eggs. He proved this idea correct by forming a hypothesis, designing an experiment, and analyzing the data.

 Scientists work in many fields and don't always answer their questions in the same way. An astronomer will investigate questions about the design of the universe in a way that will differ from a chemist trying to discover the structure of matter. Some scientists conduct experimental studies while others rely on observations and interviews. The methods scientists use to gather data depend on the questions they are trying to answer.

 With more than 130 million items, the Library of Congress in Washington, D.C., is the largest library in the world. Instead of strolling through the library's 530 miles (853 kilometers) of bookshelves, researchers often browse materials on their own computer. Like many libraries today, many of the Library of Congress' resources are available on the Internet.

 Scientists often test large experiments on miniature models. In the early 1900s, inventors Wilbur and Orville Wright tested more than 200 miniature airplane wings inside their 16-inch (41-centimeter) wide wind tunnel. After finding the best design, the inventors built full-size versions of the wings. On December 17, 1903, their wings made history as part of the first powered airplane to take flight.

Each year, hundreds of young scientists compete at the International Science and Engineering Fair (ISEF). As the largest science competition for students, ISEF judges must choose from the best science projects in the world. In 2006, they awarded $4 million in scholarships and prizes to the top competitors.

 Aquanauts experiment inside *Aquarius*, but scientists studying space head to the *International Space Station*. This giant series of modules orbits 250 miles (400 kilometers) above the earth. Scientists from around the globe, including U.S. astronauts, use the station as a laboratory and observatory.

## MORE ABOUT

### SUPER SCIENTIST

**Real name:** Maxwell J. Axiom
**Hometown:** Seattle, Washington
**Height:** 6' 1"    **Weight:** 192 lbs
**Eyes:** Brown    **Hair:** None

**Super capabilities:** Super intelligence; able to shrink to the size of an atom; sunglasses give x-ray vision; lab coat allows for travel through time and space.

**Origin:** Since birth, Max Axiom seemed destined for greatness. His mother, a marine biologist, taught her son about the mysteries of the sea. His father, a nuclear physicist and volunteer park ranger, schooled Max on the wonders of earth and sky.

One day on a wilderness hike, a megacharged lightning bolt struck Max with blinding fury. When he awoke, Max discovered a newfound energy and set out to learn as much about science as possible. He traveled the globe earning degrees in every aspect of the field. Upon his return, he was ready to share his knowledge and new identity with the world. He had become Max Axiom, Super Scientist.

# GLOSSARY

analyze (AN-uh-lize) — to examine something carefully in order to understand it

aquanaut (AK-wuh-nawt) — a scuba diver who lives and works inside and outside an underwater shelter for an extended period

conclusion (kuhn-KLOO-shuhn) — a decision or realization based on the facts available

controlled variable (kuhn-TROHLD VAIR-ee-uh-buhl) — a part of an experiment that stays the same

data (DAY-tuh) — information or facts

dependent variable (dee-PEN-duhnt VAIR-ee-uh-buhl) — a measured result of a change in the independent variable of an experiment

evidence (EV-uh-duhnss) — information, items, and facts that help prove something is true or false

hypothesis (hye-POTH-uh-siss) — a prediction that can be tested about how a scientific investigation or experiment will turn out

independent variable (in-di-PEN-duhnt VAIR-ee-uh-buhl) — a part of an experiment that changes

observation (ob-zur-VAY-shuhn) — something that you have noticed by watching carefully

prediction (pri-DIK-shuhn) — a statement of what you think will happen in the future; a hypothesis is a scientific prediction.

procedure (pruh-SEE-jur) — a set way of doing something

research (REE-surch) — to study and learn about a subject

# READ MORE

Bardhan-Quallen, Sudipta. *Last-Minute Science Fair Projects: When Your Bunsen's Not Burning but the Clock's Really Ticking.* New York: Sterling, 2006.

Carey, Stephen S. *A Beginner's Guide to Scientific Method.* Belmont, Calif.: Thomson/Wadsworth, 2004.

Harris, Elizabeth Snoke. *First Place Science Fair Projects for Inquisitive Kids.* New York: Lark Books, 2005.

Jerome, Kate Boehm. *Thinking It Through.* Math Behind the Science. Washington, D.C.: National Geographic Society, 2004.

Rosinsky, Natalie M. *How Scientists Work.* Simply Science. Minneapolis: Compass Point Books, 2004.

# INTERNET SITES

FactHound offers a safe, fun way to find Internet sites related to this book. All of the sites on FactHound have been researched by our staff.

Here's how:
1. Visit *www.facthound.com*
2. Choose your grade level.
3. Type in this book ID **1429613297** for age-appropriate sites. You may also browse subjects by clicking on letters, or by clicking on pictures and words.
4. Click on the **Fetch It** button.

**FactHound will fetch the best sites for you!**

# INDEX